A
Guide
to
Licensing
Artwork

• *Kent Press* •
Stamford, Connecticut

A Guide *to* Licensing Artwork

MARILYN MOORE

Kent Communications, Ltd.
P.O. Box 1169
Stamford, CT 06904-1169

Publisher's Cataloging in Publication

Moore, Marilyn,
A guide to licensing artwork / Marilyn Moore.
p. cm.
Includes index.
ISBN: 1-888206-03-9 (pbk)
ISBN: 1-888206-02-0 (hc)

1. Artists--Legal status, laws, etc.--United States. 2.
Law and art--United States. 3. License agreements--
United States. 4. Copyright--Art--United States. I.
Title

KF390.A7J46 1996   343.73'07
                                    QBI96-20397

About the Author

Greeting cards, gifts, illustrated books and stationery have been the focus of Marilyn Moore's product development specialties for over twenty years. In 1984, she joined The C.R. Gibson Company in Norwalk, Connecticut as Vice-President and Director of Publishing. Ms. Moore was promoted to Vice-President and Publisher in 1986. In that position, she developed a niche marketing position for greeting cards based on small collections featuring favored artists.

Ms. Moore is currently Director of Publishing for Thomas Nelson Gifts and President of Marilyn Moore & Associates, an independent consulting firm in Weston, Connecticut, which specializes in publishing services, product development and licensing. As a publishing consultant and licensing agent, she has worked with countless artists, negotiated thousands of contracts and has acquired years of experience in representing both sides of the negotiating table around the world.

Ms. Moore is a member of the Licensing Industry Merchandisers' Association ("LIMA"). She served for five years on the Judges Panel of the Louie Awards sponsored by the Greeting Cards Association ("GCA") and is a member of the Connecticut Press Club. She is the author of **Formerly Married, How to Live With Yourself,** published by Westminster Press and Berkley/Jove paperbacks and has authored numerous articles which have appeared in *Working Woman, New Woman* and *McCalls.*

v

Contents

Preface

It was yet another trade show in New York City. As publisher of a major gift and stationery company, I had been meeting with customers and industry colleagues since the early morning hours. Our company was showcasing its new line of stationery and gift products that featured original patterns and designs, new character licenses, illustrations and color trends. The line had been painstakingly worked and worried over for the past twelve months. Each item represented the creative talent, marketing savvy and manufacturing ingenuity of scores of art directors, color separators, design engineers, printers and manufacturers. Now we were testing it on the trade. The booth was teeming with wholesale buyers, chain store executives, publicists, shopkeepers, reporters, editors and marketers.

It was during all this activity and confusion that a hopeful artist asked to see me and show me her work. I felt frustrated by her request. No appointment . . . wrong time . . . wrong place. Couldn't she see we were busy? How could anyone seriously review her work when taken by surprise in this atmosphere? I explained as kindly as I could that this was not the time to show her work. She left reluctantly, dragging her heavy portfolio with her. Watching her sad retreating figure, I wondered then what artistic riches might be stored in that bulging folder and, if indeed there were riches, how they would ever find their way into the marketplace with such representation.

That is what this book is about. How to get your work out of your portfolio. It is about how to take your art off the wall and into the commercial world. In essence, it is about how to license your art.

In this book, I will share with you the insights, experiences and advice gleaned from numerous artists, manufacturers and licensing representatives. The book will discuss making presentations, meeting your potential client's needs and protecting your rights. While these ideas are commonly endorsed by publishers, manufacturers, artists and agents alike, the advice is my own, shaped by my twenty-five years of product development in the publishing and gift industries.

The draft agreements in the Appendix are only for you to familiarize yourself with the legal issues and points of law that you can expect to encounter in a licensing agreement. If you try to adapt them for your own use, please remember that each manufacturer, product category, distribution channel and market segment has certain standards and practices that are peculiar to only it. There is no single preprinted agreement that can serve every situation. The terms of each agreement that you enter into will be a reflection of the particular understanding that you and your client have reached regarding *one* particular piece of art for *one* particular use, in *one* particular market at *one* particular time.

Many persons have shared their expertise and experience with me in the preparation of this book. Shirley Henschel, President of Alaska Momma, a licensing company; Gail Levites, Design Consultant; Hans Wilhelm, internationally licensed illustrator; and Wendy Seiffer, President of Wendy Seiffer Associates have been generous with anecdotes and advice. Gregory J. Battersby of Grimes and Battersby in Stamford, Connecticut provided legal guidance and the sample agreements for the Appendices. Michelle Lostaglio was a supportive editor and researcher. I thank them all for their help.

It is my hope that you will find here some encouraging and realistic advice that you can use to take your art off the wall and get it onto a variety of income-producing products.

Marilyn Moore

One:
You and Your Art

Most artists are very sensitive about their own creativity. Why shouldn't they be? They have to survive the rigors of training, the assault of criticism and the loneliness of solitary work. Artists have every right to feel protective of their work. They have exposed a portion of their souls in each work that they create. Each new work reflects a particular insight or some way of seeing and understanding that is unique and personal to the artist. With time, prospects of some financial gain and a healthy disinterest give some artists the ability to release their proprietary hold and be objective and critical of their work. Others will always remain emotionally connected and unable to let go.

Self-Analysis: The First Step

Before deciding to enter the licensing arena, you should ask yourself several questions about you and your art. Complete honesty is essential.

You may be embarking on an endeavor for which you are not suited — an endeavor that might demoralize you, damage your creativity or divert you from your artistic calling. On the other hand, you may find yourself on a path to an exciting creative process that can bring you great financial and artistic rewards, heightened creativity and a new career! The following questions can help you find out if you fit the commercial artist profile.

• Are you willing to let go of your art? Letting go — or putting your work into someone else's hands — is true surrender. The extent to which you are willing to exploit your work and the level of control you feel you need to protect your work are pertinent issues to consider before entering the commercial world. Presumably, your canvasses were painted to hang on the wall. Will you be offended if your painting is reproduced on coffee mugs, wall calendars and shower curtains? It is best to explore your personal emotional limits as an artist before you let your "babies" leave home and fend for themselves. It will also save you from later embarrassments and regrets.

• Can you accept commercial standards of reproduction? The craft of transforming a single piece of art into a run of mass-produced greeting cards, linens, book jackets or porcelain plates is painstakingly difficult. Each medium has its own standard of "commercially acceptable quality." If you compare the colors in an original painting with its reproduction on a commercial product, you might be surprised by the contrasts. The differences can be due to printers' ink tolerances, color separating techniques, material absorption and manufacturing limitations. Reputable and successful manufacturers do strive for quality reproduction and make every effort to get as close to the original as possible. Finding and then settling for an acceptable reproduction quality in certain product categories can be essential to your ongoing relationships with manufacturers.

• Will you create more for a client and will you deliver on time? Licensing agents, art directors and manufacturers do respect your calling as an artist. They know that it takes time, inspiration and motivation to create. But when you put yourself into the licensing arena, you are opening yourself up to potential commitments that may require grueling work and back-breaking deadlines. A single piece of art may be so popular as a licensed property that the manufacturer will want to create a series, expand the line or commission a particular subject matter. The artist's cooperation is vital to the ongoing success of the business.

• Can you take criticism, direction and rejection without taking it personally? Art directors and product developers have no-nonsense jobs. If your art doesn't fit their product requirements, they can't use it. It does not matter that your painting won a blue ribbon in a juried show; or that your neighbor thinks it would make a beautiful greeting card; or that the work of art took more of your time, more of your heart and more of your skill than anything you have ever created before. If it doesn't fit, it doesn't work. The art director may dismiss it because the dimensions are wrong. The product manager may tell you that your themes are unsuitable or that your style is overdone or unpopular. You can listen. You can learn. You can adapt. But don't take this kind of rejection as a personal reflection on your talent and ability as an artist.

• Can your art stand the scrutiny of the professional eye? You do have a responsibility to be objective about your work. Some pieces are well-executed. Others might be sketchy and not fully realized. When you prepare to show your work, it is important that you understand that it will be subjected to critical evaluation. Are the colors clean? Are the lines pure? Have you achieved the level of skill that would be expected from a professional who works in the style and medium you have chosen? Your ability to be consistent in your work is important. Nothing is more disappointing than when a product manager is attracted to a particular work only to discover that it is a "lucky accident." In this case, the artist cannot produce more work of similar quality because his skill is not sufficiently developed.

• Does your art have a broad appeal? Shirley Henschel, president of Alaska Momma, Inc., a licensing company, successfully represents a select number of artists to manufacturers of consumer products. Calendars, greeting cards, housewares, home furnishings, games, linens and apparel are just a few of the product categories that bear the work of her clients. "To put together a good licensing program, I want art that has broad consumer appeal," she says. Shirley meets with leading manufacturers at their offices and in her own in New York City as well as at the numerous industry shows she attends throughout the year. "The art should be in color; black and white is too limiting. And the art should be representational. Abstract art is just not accessible. I find that often illustration is more effective than fine art because it tells a story. Fine art can be harder to sell."

Self Expression vs. Mass Appeal

The art world is filled with many works of self-expression. It fills our art galleries and graces our homes. Many artists express their deepest feelings and relive their most meaningful experiences through the medium of their choosing. We respond to the emotional content and the symbolism. We value it because of its unique and singular expression of a mood, an idea, a place and a person.

Art that is best suited for licensing has different criteria. Perhaps from its very inception it was created to appeal to others. The theme is clear; the content is recognizable. The images — figurative, illustrative, symbolic and decorative — are popular with the consumer and appropriate to the product on which they appear.

Two:
Analyzing Your Work

Before you approach an art director or product manager about licensing your art, it is a good idea to analyze your work for its application, practicality and adaptability. Regardless of its content, theme and artistic execution, you must be sure that it can actually be reproduced without undo effort and expense on the part of the manufacturer. Perhaps you have already secured professionally prepared slides or transparencies of your work — slides that are true to the color, tones and textures of your original work. Most manufacturers will work from this reproductive form to design their products, without ever touching the original work.

Releasing and Reproducing Your Art

Can you release your original work to the manufacturer so that it can be photographically or digitally scanned? Some applications require that the original be available. There is always the risk of unintentional damage or shopwear to the original work. Can you accept that as a possibility? Even if you are willing to release the original art, some manufacturers and many licensing agents insist on working with color transparencies. The responsibility of protecting original work is too great a burden for them.

However you solve the issue of reproduction, it is something you will want to address before you begin to pursue any licensing transaction. The art on the wall is of no value as a license if it cannot be practically reproduced for manufacture. The artist's role is to understand the various manufacturers' requirements and to provide them with art in a form that is usable, adaptable and reproducible.

Getting a Handle on Your Style

Once you have determined how your art can be reproduced, you can begin to assess its style. If you have worked in a variety of styles, you may want to organize and present your work in those style groups. The medium you work in is one defining attribute. Watercolor, gouache, oil, acrylic or collage — each represents a different approach to the subject matter and a different expectation in the eye of the art director.

It is also useful to be able to describe your work as briefly and as quickly as possible. In other words, you need to have a verbal handle on your work. Does it represent a particular "school" such as French Impressionism or Old Master? Might one be able to use a well-known painter's name in association with your work? Is it in the style of Monet? Or does it evoke Georgia O'Keeffe or Keith Haring? These questions are not to suggest that your work needs to be in someone else's style to be successful, but if it is reminiscent of a style, it can be helpful to point that out.

Several years ago I needed a new greeting card line for a stationery company. We had published whimsical bears and bunnies, pretty florals, Victorian collage, cartoons and characters. When a licensing agent called for an appointment to show me some new "floral" work I agreed to see her. But with little eagerness. Who needed more flowers?

She came into the conference room and laid out a series of transparencies featuring lush, beautiful gardens — deep greens, soft mauves and blues, roses and reds, huge oil paintings of gardens in bloom that evoked the spirit of the French Impressionists. I gasped. Recently there had been an important touring art show of the French Impressionists. The art style was enjoying a surge in popularity and was currently featured in home furnishings, framed prints and posters. This artist's work was "in the style of" those Impressionists! And there was an abundance of images to choose from.

I negotiated a license to the work, creating a line of greeting cards called "Secret Gardens." We billed the work as "museum quality Impressionist paintings in the style of Monet." The line was an instant hit and the agent went on to secure licenses for the artist in housewares, stationery, photo albums, diaries, journals and gift wrappings — all developed around this look of the Impressionists. That is the value of having a "handle" on your style.

Recurring Themes

Certain recurring themes and subject matter can direct you to appropriate products and manufacturers. Through-the-year landscapes and horoscopes suggest calendars. Regional images such as Southwestern desert flowers or New England seascapes may suggest a series of collectible plates or playing cards. Infants and juvenile themes suggest appropriate products. If you catalogue your work by subject matter, the process may lead you to consideration of the types of products that would be most suitable for your work.

A key to success in this process of evaluation is determining in which categories you have sufficient quantity to actually make a presentation. One or two paintings in a few categories are not enough to introduce you to the licensing world. You may sell an image here and there, or you may hook up with a company that will assign you some work.

But to actively pursue the licensing business, you will usually need a critical mass of art in a style or theme that a manufacturer can work with and develop into a line of products. When your work is presented to a manufacturer, product manager or licensing agent, it should demonstrate through its quantity and consistency that a particular piece of art is not a one-of-a-kind lucky accident of creativity. Most manufacturers are thinking about the next *line*, not the next *item*. What trend can they create . . . or follow? Where will they find the art to make it happen? When they consider your work they will need to know that there is enough of it to create a product line and to meet the market's demand. The consistency of style or theme demonstrates that you have control of your materials and subject matter and that you can deliver additional work, if necessary, in a similar style.

Recognizing Your Art's Strengths and Weaknesses

This personal analysis of your work, prior to exposing it to the licensing industry, is suggested to you as a way of protecting yourself from embarrassment and disappointment. To be successful licensors, artists need to do their homework. You should try to be objective about your work, to look at it from a manufacturer's point of view and see it as the commodity it might become. As you learn to recognize and accept the specific positive attributes of your art (as well as its limitations) you will build self-confidence that is borne out of the security of knowing what you are doing and why. Some work is better suited to license than others. Some artists are better suited to the licensing business than others. Self-understanding will help you determine your role in the business.

THREE:
Analyzing the Products

It can be a burden to be an artist. You study and work in a field that is sometimes scorned for being impractical or self-indulgent. Parents worry that their artist child will not make a living; educators hastily abandon art instruction as "unnecessary" when public school budgets are strained; and public support for the arts is a political football. Yet you persist as an artist, developing your gifts and practicing your talent in spite of little encouragement, faint praise and meager financial gain. If only you had been born with an accountant's skill or an engineer's talent!

The Commercial Artist in Today's Marketplace

The good news is that in spite of the seeming devaluation of artists in our society, never has art been so vital and valuable to the flow of new and attractive consumer products into the marketplace. Look about your home. Your furniture, table linens, paper goods, textiles, utensils and accessories all have been enhanced with the added value of the touch of an artist's hand.

The computerized technological advances of the 1990's have greatly simplified the process of reproducing art for the purpose of mass manufacturing. Art can be digitally scanned and converted into three dimensions. Colors can be enhanced or altered to match existing products. Images can be transmitted from originals to finished products, while being stored and manipulated within the labyrinthine workings of a computerized work station. This technological revolution has created a huge appetite for art in the marketplace. Successful consumer products result from the creativity of those who have mastered the *possible* and the *practical.* New possibilities create demand. New practicalities permit choice and variety. The result is more products, more designs, more style and more choices. Consider something as simple as a plate. *One* plate. But a thousand different art styles and images on a thousand different plates transform *one* product into *one thousand* products. Herein lies many exciting opportunities for the commercial artist.

Searching Product Categories That Complement Your Art

What art have you already created that might be appropriate for certain products? Study the objects in your home. Imagine your art adapted as decorative elements in the manufacture of those objects. Is your art appropriate for the function of the object? For instance, the function of a greeting card is to communicate. Art themes that impede that function of communication are not appropriate to the product. Products in the kitchen or dining room should not detract from the aesthetic of preparing and eating food. Will your art enhance the appeal of the object? Manufacturers apply art to their products because they believe that it will increase sales. Appropriately decorated products have added perceived value. The key word here is appropriate.

Look at the products in your home and analyze what it is that prompted you to buy them for your personal use. Was it a color scheme? A popular image? Does the item communicate something about your gender, age, personality, taste or income level? The more you can read the mind of consumers (and you are one, too), the more you will understand the emotions that drive their choices, and the easier it will be for you to position your work in the marketplace and sell it for certain product categories.

Learning to Meet Design Requirements

Some products have particular design requirements that make certain art styles impractical. For example, most gift wraps, wall covering and textiles utilize step-and-repeat patterns so that the design is repeated in a geometric form, giving the impression of an all-over design. Knowing how to engineer your work, knowing when your work can or cannot be manipulated to meet design requirements and having a few alternative solutions to design and engineering problems are skills that you will find helpful as you consider product categories for your existing work and when you plan and create new art in the future.

Seeking Out Potential Manufacturers

The Appendices contain a list of manufacturers of various products. This is a good starting point. Look for these manufacturer's products in the market, see the kinds of art they have licensed and compare their products with competitive products. Do you have a look or style that would give the manufacturer a competitive edge? As you come to understand products from the manufacturer's point of view, you will be able to position your art and develop new art that can meet the manufacturer's objectives.

Understanding the Risks of the Manufacturer

Manufacturers, their product managers and art directors like to work with artists who understand their problems and are willing to help solve them. Developing a new line is risky. All of the market research, analysis and product testing in the world cannot guarantee a successful and profitable launch of a new product. Product managers literally put their jobs on the line when they launch new products. The art director is also risking his or her professional reputation and a great deal of the manufacturer's money. The artist takes the smallest risk of all. Presuming you will be paid at least a minimum amount for your time and effort as an advance against royalties, you have received compensation. Thereafter, if the project fails in the marketplace, you may not get rich on royalties, but you won't have lost any money either. The manufacturer, on the other hand, loses all. The art development expense for a modest new gift line can run into the hundreds of thousands of dollars. Every manufacturer is gambling with that kind of money. Their investment will not be recouped until well after the artist's advance has been earned back, and the product has sold through the marketing chain to the consumer.

As a consequence of these risks, financial and otherwise, manufacturers appreciate artists who are willing to "partner" with them. Artists who are sensitive to the risks involved will not make unreasonable demands, will cooperate in all of the phases of the product development process and will be a team player with the manufacturer's staff.

There are many opportunities for you to reap substantial rewards for well-designed products. Your partnership with the product development team will help ensure that you will receive your reward.

FOUR:
Analyzing the Markets

The word "market" evokes images of teeming village squares with open air stands — vendors hawking their wares, fresh produce, livestock, crafts people and artisans vying for the villagers' attention and money. Market Day was important to the life of Early American villages because this "market" made it possible for the residents to select from a variety of sources, those goods (essential and nonessential) that sustained and enriched their daily life. There was also an occasional itinerant tradesman — the knife sharpener, the blacksmith, the seamstress — who brought products directly to the home. The market for products was simple and direct. Everyone shopped in the same place from the same vendors for the same products.

Defining the Marketplace

Today, there are a vast number of markets for selling products. Downtown Main Street, with a few rugged independent retailers selling to a pedestrian population, might most resemble the historic village market. Department stores and national chain stores draw a different and more mobile customer and offer a wider variety of products, often with their "own-store" private label branding. Mass-market super stores attract bargain-hunters who will exchange service for economy. There are highly focused markets such as museum stores and specialty gift shops; there are mail markets, television markets and electronic markets; there are markets that are defined by consumer taste and style; there are markets that are defined by product category and there are markets that are defined by price level.

Targeting Specific Markets

Each market has its own criteria for successful products. Consumer lifestyle, age, education and income do influence product selection. What is popular in fashion, design trends, style and form will vary from market to market. Successful manufacturers know which markets they are successful in, where they want to expand and what markets to avoid. They will design their products to meet those marketing goals.

Simply put, "marketing" is a discipline or technique utilized by manufacturers which attempts to understand and even influence the needs and desires of the customers in a particular market and to subsequently bring to the marketplace products that will fill those needs.

What does all of the above have to do with you? Plenty. In today's manufacturing companies, product managers are increasingly directed by marketing experts in their art and design selections. An art director's personal taste and sensibilities are not necessarily the defining criteria. Product development has become an objective process of analysis, forecasting, test marketing and decision-by-committee. Creativity and inspiration are encouraged and valued, but those impulses are contained within the larger mechanism of the marketing dynamic.

Understanding the Product Development Chain

If the artist can understand the product development chain within a given company and the factors that will influence art and design decisions, the artist will be better prepared to make an appropriate presentation. Too often, artists feel personal and professional rejection when their art is rejected by a potential licensee. It is important to remember that sometimes the negative response has nothing to do with the quality of the art or the artist. It is the market discipline that shapes the decision. So the more the artist learns about where a particular art style will be placed in the marketing world, the better prepared the artist will be for the presentation, discussion, acceptance or rejection of his or her work.

Keeping Up With Market Trends

Read Trade and Consumer Publications

As you become aware of the marketing influences that shape product development, you will be able to use consumer magazines to inform yourself about marketing trends. You will perceive that readers of *Ladies Home Journal* may be a different market than the readers of *Town and Country.* They will shop in different stores and they will respond to different style trends. Where does your art fit in these markets? Read the consumer magazines for fashion suggestions, color preferences and style changes.

Trade magazines targeted to the industries that feature licensed art will keep you informed about what is going on in the industry, and the business decisions that shape product lines. *Gift and Stationery Business, Gift and Decorative Accessories, Greetings, HFD (Home Furnishings Directory)* and *WomensWear Daily* are a few of the magazines that will educate the reader about popular trends and marketing directions.

Magazines targeted to the licensing industry, such as *The Licensing Journal* and *The Licensing*

Book, inform readers of new developments and opportunities in licensing.

Observe Current Events and Societal Trends

Current events, the political climate, social issues and popular culture have an influence on product design and art selection. Marketing directors try to read the mind of the consumer and develop products that will stir positive responses.

The first Earth Day, a public demonstration of concern for saving the planet, was held in 1970. This was the beginning of the popularization of "environmental issues" as a social and political concern rather than a purely scientific concern. By the 1990's those same "environmental issues" had evolved into a market position and a design style!

Popular demand for recycled paper and forest preservation spawned new standards for paper goods, resulting in rough-textured stocks and off-white papers. Concern for endangered species prompted a search for artistic representations of wildlife and nature in all its forms. Greeting cards and stationery carried politically correct messages to save the earth, preserve the rain forest, protect our rivers or support the world wildlife. What began as a scientific concern so captured the public's imagination that a new consumer market developed.

This "environmental-friendly" market created many opportunities for botanical painters, landscape artists, zoological artists and any artists that could execute fine art representations of the flora and fauna of our world. Many artists whose work had previously been perceived as only suitable for framed prints and museum shops found new venues for their talent in the popular application of "nature art" to a vast array of products, including wall coverings, linens, books, apparel, stationery, posters and prints.

Of course, while this "nature trend" as a design statement will not last forever, the core consumers for "earth-friendly" designs will remain. But the next popular idea will sweep the masses along on a new wave to the latest trend. It is important to remember that all fashion trends have their own life cycle. Angels, heavenly bodies and astrological symbols all had their design genesis in the popular culture. New-Age spirituality fueled an interest in crystals, mythical beings, candles and incense. The 1990's have been called the age of "cocooning," spurring an interest in a stay-at-home lifestyle, emphasizing finely prepared meals, warmly elegant home furnishings and traditional fine art accessories.

All of these fashion directions did not emerge from a vacuum. They were shaped out of the emotional, social and political climate as documented in our daily newspapers and television. Be aware of current events and observe how they can shape our culture, instruct our taste and inform our senses. You may be able to see the next design trend.

Browse the Marketplace: Go Shopping

No amount of theory can replace the actual experience of the retail environment. Browse the gift shops, department stores and boutiques. Peruse catalogues and study fashion advertising. Take note of the price differences for products in different stores. Note the differing design preferences, color pallets, themes and subject categories. You are seeing different lifestyle marketing. Ask yourself where your work would look best. Where would it have the most appeal? Which retail store carries products that look compatible with your art style? Which products would be enhanced by your work? The answers to these questions can tell you what market segments to go after and which manufacturers to target. The manufacturers that are already producing similar art could be prospects for a presentation of your artwork.

It is also important to talk to shop keepers. They will probably welcome the opportunity to present their opinions about style and trends. They will alert you to which manufacturers seem to be in financial trouble, which give poor service, which are reliable and steady and who's hot and who's not. These independent retailers, the buyers who select the merchandise for their stores, are the first and most important customers for licensed products. An artist might create the world's most gorgeous and trendy line of products, but if the retailer won't buy it from the manufacturer, it will never be bought by the consumer. Listen to the retailers and pay heed to their counsel.

Attend Trade Shows

Throughout the year, in every region of the country, there are industry specific trade shows for retailers and marketers to view the manufacturers' new lines and to order their merchandise. A schedule of the major U.S. trade shows is included in the Appendices to this book. These shows are not usually open to the general public and require a business card or similar identification of trade affiliation for attendance.

Try to attend a few of these shows in your area. Just walking the aisles and observing the products and their designs will give you a good sense of what is going on in the industry. Often the trade show will sponsor educational seminars on licensing, marketing and product development. These seminars can be extremely helpful. You will become more familiar with the vocabulary of the industry, get to know some of the significant players in the field and acquire some of the nuts and bolts information that can help you do business in a professional manner. Once you have come to know some of the people in the industry, you can make inquiries about on-site meetings and appointments. But always remain sensitive to the manufacturer's primary purpose for being at a trade show. His purpose is to sell products. Any interference with the manufacturer's process of displaying and selling products to buyers will not be appreciated and will not be forgotten.

Trade shows do provide an opportunity for artists to network. Working as an artist can be solitary and lonely. Making connections with other artists who are also trying to crack into the licensing business can be very helpful and supportive. Sharing ideas, suggestions and encouragement with fellow artists can give you and your career just the right boost. Friendships that are forged through mutually-shared professional interests are valuable and lasting.

Licensing clients enjoy working with artists who are willing to help with their marketing problems. Buying a new design and preparing the art for production is costly. Product managers, art directors and marketing managers take big risks with their company's resources. Every decision they make puts their professional credibility and their careers at risk. A mistaken design direction can cause a company to lose not only sales dollars, but its competitive position in the marketplace.

An artist who is knowledgeable of marketing issues, aware of the risks involved and willing to be a partner in the product development process will be in a good position to forge healthy and long-term relationships with licensees.

FIVE:
Preparing for the Presentation

You've decided to give licensing a try. Now it's time to get organized. A professional presentation will demonstrate that you know what you are doing and that you understand and respect what your potential client wants to do. Your presentation should require little explanation and no apology. It should be rationally put together, attractive and thorough. It should convey your own confidence in your work and your mastery of your style.

At this point, the content of your work is well-executed. The work is original and appropriate. But presentation is an important step in licensing your artwork, equally important as the work itself. A fine chef's entree loses its appeal if it is presented on an unattractive serving dish. A distinguished watercolor can be devalued by an ugly color matte and poor framing. Likewise, the artist's portfolio, simple and professional, should enhance — not detract from — the work.

Formatting the Work

It may be a good idea to have a respected commercial photographer take professional slides or transparencies of the artwork. If possible, have some color laser photocopies made also. If original unframed unformed work can be shown, gather a few representative pieces. If some of your work has been commercially printed, collect a few samples. These will demonstrate how your work reproduces on a saleable product. Promotion pieces — catalogue pages, promotional fliers, advertising — serve not only to showcase your work, but add a little subliminal advertising of yourself to the client.

Determining the Scope of the Presentation

How much work should you be prepared to show? When Gail Levites was Design Director of a major gift and stationery company, she would tell artists, "Don't edit!!! You can't possibly know everything that's in my mind! I don't even know everything that's in my mind! If I see it I'll say, 'Yes, that's what I've been looking for!'" Because her company produced so many different categories of products — paper tableware, stationery, photo albums, illustrated books, gift wrap, greeting cards, journals — her art needs were broad and eclectic. Gail also knows that some artists have mastered several media and styles. They may neglect to show earlier, accomplished work in favor of their current style. "Bring it all!" she says. "I want to see your range as well as your skill."

Other companies may have a single product line such as greeting cards. They want to see only that which is category specific. A few mockups with color laser reproductions to show how the art would translate into a product or product line can be an effective showcase to add to your portfolio.

Organizing the Presentation

The key to an effective presentation, whether broad in scope or very specific, is organization. Try to formulate some kind of rationale for your portfolio that can be understood when you are not there to interpret it. Have you created a series of images that hold together as a line? Or do you have a body of work that is in a particular medium, such as oil or watercolor? Do you have some tightly rendered images that contrast with a loose impressionistic style? Again, if you have made some rough translations of art into product applications, include them where appropriate. Anything that you can do in the organization of your portfolio that will tell a visual story about you and your work will be an important selling tool for you. If your presentation is primarily with slides, it would be good if you could include a few original pieces of art for the initial visual impact so that an art director can see firsthand how you execute your work.

Selling Yourself

It is a good idea to compose a short bio or curriculum vitae with pertinent information that would impact favorably on a potential licensee. Art education, employment in related design fields, retail experience, teachers, mentors and references — this information can position you as knowledgeable in the field. Always include a list of past and current licensees, self-published products and their brand names, designers you have worked with and any significant sales figures. Keep this list up to date for easy reference and as a check against conflicts of use.

Always include some kind of hand out or "leave with" material that can be kept on file as a sample of your work with telephone and address for future reference. Color photocopies are an inexpensive means of accomplishing this.

The Interview or Presentation

With your presentation organized in a binder or portfolio, you are ready to start making rounds. Even if a potential licensee is around the corner from where you live, always telephone or write first to request an interview. Do not drop in unexpectedly. In an initial phone call you can ask about the company's portfolio review policy, the names and titles of the significant decision makers and the timing for art selection as it relates to manufacturing schedules.

If a manufacturer will give you an interview and it is practical for you to meet, by all means take advantage of the opportunity. This might be at a trade show (if you have made arrangements in advance) or at the company's offices. Be prepared. Prior to your interview, remember to familiarize yourself with the breadth of the company's product lines. I continue to be amazed at the number of artists who will manage to secure appointments with art directors and product managers yet who will not bother to find out the range of their product lines and the extent of licensed work that is utilized. It is exactly this kind of information that can help you converse intelligently and sympathetically during your interview.

Sending Your Portfolio in the Mail

If you are denied a meeting, you may be encouraged to mail your portfolio. Be sure to get the exact name of the addressee. A cover letter to that person is absolutely essential. In it you will briefly introduce yourself, summarize a few highlights from your curriculum vitae and set a time — a few weeks to a month — when you will make a follow-up call. You will also include a self-addressed postage paid envelope or express mail form so that your portfolio can be safely returned to you.

Copyright Concerns

Some artists fear that their designs will be copied by unscrupulous manufacturers. Some artists fear that releasing their portfolios to potential manufacturers risks losing their copyright protection. But the work is protected. Under the law of the Berne Convention, to which the United States and most countries throughout the world are signatories, copyright protection commences upon the creation of any tangible work. It does not even require that a copyright notice be posted on the work. And you can register a copyright with the U.S. Copyright Office by filing a very simple form. An example of this form is found in the Appendices. More information on copyright protection can be found in Chapter Eight of this work.

Of more frequent concern is the vulnerability of manufacturers to suits brought by artists who claim design theft. Companies that maintain design studios have design concepts in process continuously. There can be a universal style trend that will be created and interpreted independently by countless artists at a given time. Licensing professionals are aware of this synchronicity. Less experienced artists, seeing a design similar to their own in the marketplace, may accuse a manufacturer of copyright violation, assuming that the studio was inspired by the contents of their rejected portfolio.

Release Forms: Protection for the Manufacturer

To protect themselves from the necessity of defending against frivolous lawsuits, some companies will not see an artist's portfolio unless the artist, prior to the portfolio submission, signs a release form. This document asks the artist to acknowledge that the artwork submitted may be similar in form and content to artwork currently being developed in the manufacturer's studio; that while the artist's work is original, the ideas contained within it are not necessarily new and that the artist is submitting work with the full knowledge that the manufacturer may in the future introduce product bearing images similar to the form and content of the submitted work with no obligation or responsibility to the submitting artist. If the artist refuses to sign the release, the portfolio will be refused and returned unopened.

These are tough terms for the artist to absorb. However, in most cases, it is in the artist's best interest to sign the release form if it will grant the artist and the portfolio an audience with the company. With all of the artwork that they see, manufacturers are troubled by confidentiality issues and copyright challenges. There is always a chance that an independent artist's work will turn out to be similar to something that the manufacturer has been developing internally. Manufacturers are understandably cautious about personally seeing new artists. They might feel safer working with a licensing agent or seeking out the artists through university programs, contests, competitions and aggressive recruitment plans.

Fortunately, most industry leaders are committed to fair business practices in the development of new talent. The need for new art and new artists continues. Manufacturers are constantly seeking new designs from fresh new artists. Furthermore, manufacturers are happy to pay the going rate for art that will increase their products' sales. Because many manufacturers depend on the artwork that comes from independent artists, it is unlikely that a reputable manufacturer will steal or otherwise intentionally infringe on an artist's work. Therefore, artists can feel relatively secure in releasing their portfolios under the conditions of a release form.

In conclusion, your portfolio is your letter of introduction, your calling card and your key to unlocking the doors to the very licensees who are looking for you and your work. Organizing your portfolio, keeping it up to date, adapting it to the sensibilities of a prospective licensee, keeping a balanced perspective between your needs and a licensee's concerns are the practices that will ear-mark you as a professional and that will eventually earn you the recognition you deserve.

Six:
Negotiating Terms of the License Agreement

You've organized your artwork, researched the potential manufacturer and made a concise and thorough presentation of your artwork to the product manager. What happens next? If you are fortunate, the product manager says, "Yes! It's time to negotiate!" At this point, whether you are representing yourself or working through an agent, you will want to be familiar with the essentials of a design license agreement. You will want to understand just what it is that the manufacturer wants from you and what you are agreeing to. You will need to understand what the manufacturer intends to do with your work, exactly what he will pay you for that privilege and what the payment method will be.

The Starting Point: A Verbal Agreement

During the meeting with the product manager, it is a good idea to jot down notes about who is agreeing to what and then read them back to the parties in the room before ending the conversation. This will ensure that both parties understand the essentials of the all issues involved. These notes can help you when you review the final contract. This friendly exchange, a kind of "gentleperson's verbal agreement" prior to drawing up a contract, is much of the glue that will bind the parties to the eventual legal agreement. When all is said and done, it is the *mutually* agreed-upon intentions and purposes that will make a licensing agreement succeed. The contract, then, becomes a piece of paper that simply documents what has already been agreed upon during negotiations.

Some artists are unable negotiate. They do not know how to balance their need to protect their work with their obligation to satisfy the client. In that state of mind, many artists fail to recognize opportunities to advance their careers, or, in their eagerness to please, fail to recognize the warning signs of potential abuse. In such cases, a licensing agent or an attorney who specializes in licensing and copyright issues can be helpful. Licensing agents will be discussed in Chapter Seven.

Using an Attorney

An attorney can be very helpful during the negotiation of the written contract. Using the format that follows, review your negotiations with an attorney. If the attorney is familiar with licensing issues, he or she may raise questions about the agreement and point out the ramifications of your decisions. Even attorneys who are not familiar with licensing practices can review your agreement and provide good counsel to be sure that it properly protects your interest. Attorneys with licensing experience may have opinions regarding the terms you have agreed to. This is only natural. Listen to their opinions and consider their advice. It can be truly valuable.

One very wise attorney cautions his clients: "You have to make an agreement that you are comfortable with because you want to do the work. You know how much it means to you. I can advise you, I can warn you, I can encourage you. But I can't agree for you."

Whose Form to Use

Now that you (the artist) and your licensee (the manufacturer) have come to general terms, you will want to draw up the written contract. Herein begins the battle of forms. You may be given the manufacturer's standard form agreement and asked to sign it, or you may be able to negotiate the use of your own form agreement. There is an advantage to being the party that writes the contract. There will be no buried clauses that you won't understand, the language is your own and the terms are clearly stated as *you* understand them.

Should the licensee insist on drawing the contract, you should review it with your attorney. Although you do not want to be "difficult" and convey an attitude of mistrust at the very beginning of what can be a profitable working partnership, it is important to review the contract thoroughly. Then, if your lawyer finds some troublesome language or contradictory clauses, he or she can guide you in discussing these problems with the licensee and you can feel confident that you are on firm and rational legal ground. This also give the licensee an opportunity to at least explain and justify a company policy or to eliminate the troubling language from the contract.

All of these conversations and negotiations are best conducted in an atmosphere where there is a presumption of fairness and trust. With knowledge and experience, you will find that contracts that begin under adversarial conditions are rarely productive. Knowledge is your best defense and ignorance is no defense. Your attorney can help you acquire that knowledge.

Points To Remember When Negotiating a License Agreement

Licensing is a partnership. Sensible negotiations require the ability to walk in your partner's shoes for at least a part of the time. You want to have a healthy degree of objectivity about your partner's value to you and your value to the partner, and a desire to find the path toward mutual trust and agreement.

Before you reach that point, however, it is helpful for you to know what your absolute bottom line is — not just what you want, but what you need. Do you need exposure? Cash? An introduction to a new product category? Are you overworked? Underutilized? Frantic? Bored? Having the answers to these and similar questions — knowing what your needs are and honoring them — will put you in a better position to negotiate on your own behalf while protecting your basic interests. Most licensing agreements are not difficult. Most are straightforward and clear in intent. The industry is made up of honorable people who respect your contribution to their success. They want to come to a reasonable agreement with you and get on with their work of creating products.

Basic Terms of the License Agreement

A review of the essential ingredients in a license agreement will help you make the decision that is right for you, both professionally and personally. An agreement that is good for you may be disastrous for another artist. In the same way, an agreement that is acceptable at this stage of your career may be unacceptable to you later. If you can understand the issues involved, you can at least make an informed acceptance or rejection of the offer.

The Grant

The grant of rights is where the artist (the Licensor) grants the manufacturing company (the Licensee) the *right to use* art (the Works) created by you. That is the whole essence of your agreement. *How* the manufacturer can use it, *where* he or she can use it, and the *length of time* that he or she can use it will be your areas of discussion and negotiation. The *extent* of use is the issue.

Some companies may want to buy your work outright. They will purchase the art and its copyright and subsequently own it as if they were, in fact, the creator of the art. A "work for hire" agreement requires that the artist relinquish all of his or her rights to the work in any format, as well as the copyright to the work itself. Obviously, this is the broadest extent of "use."

Some artists are paid handsomely for work for hire, particularly in high-fashion cosmetic packaging design and designer textiles. Other artists have carelessly signed away all rights to their art through ignorance or carelessness. Certainly, it would be wise for artists to put a high premium on any work for hire work agreement, if they consider it at all. Sample work for hire agreements are included in the Appendices.

The Rights

As an artist, you may grant an "all rights" agreement. Typically, this type of agreement acknowledges that the copyright is held by the artist and the actual "work" is owned by the artist. But the licensee has the right to exploit the work *in any manner.* The artist owns the actual painting but has signed away the reproduction rights. The artist cannot license the work to another manufacturer for any purpose whatsoever during the term of the agreement. In this type of agreement, the manufacturer becomes the exclusive licensee of the artwork which is the subject of the agreement.

The artist may also grant an exclusive license to the manufacturer for specific product categories. In this scenario, the licensee would be the only manufacturer for a particular product category, leaving the artist to grant other licenses for the artwork in other categories. The artist may also grant non-exclusive licenses, where in any given category, the artist may grant numerous licenses for the same artwork. Most manufacturers are reluctant to sign agreements which do not give them any form of exclusivity, due to the highly competitive nature of the manufacturing industry.

Product Categories and Market Channels

It is typically desirable for the artist to grant rights by product category. For instance, you may encounter a manufacturer specializing in stationery, greeting cards and wall calendars. Another party manufactures placemats, dishtowels and pot holders. Still another publishes journals and notebooks. Each manufacturer wants reproduction rights to your art, but only for the product categories in which they manufacture. As the licensor, you may grant licenses for the same piece of art to each of these manufacturers, granting each exclusive use of the artwork in their category for the term of the agreement. This is a smart way to approach licensing as it allows the artist to build recognition for the artwork in various categories. Some artists make the mistake of granting one manufacturer a broad range of product categories. This often does not allow the artist to receive full recognition in the marketplace, because few manufacturers can manufacture products in all the applicable categories. Therefore, it is advisable for the artist to structure the license agreement so that each manufacturer is granted the rights to reproduce the artwork only on the types of products that he or she can bring to market.

Some licensors are able to further refine the extent of use by defining the specific markets where the products will be sold. A manufacturer may sell bookmarks to the mass market only, or through catalogue sales only, leaving the independent retailing and department store distribution to a different manufacturer. The art can then be redesigned and used in a different style by another licensee for that same product in a different market. This practice is common in the licensing of animated television and movie characters. Nevertheless, it is wise, if possible, to define the market in which the licensed products will be sold and to reserve any rights that will not be exploited by the manufacturer.

Territory

Some companies distribute only in their own country. Others have the ability to distribute globally. It is important for the artist to know up front what the licensee's distribution capabilities are. Granting rights to a licensee for a territory that the licensee cannot reach, or withholding rights for a territory that you cannot personally exploit are equally foolish moves. Many companies are expanding their international trade, and most artists will want their licensed product to participate in that growth. But if the artist already has a foreign business connection that is interested in the artwork, the territory provision in the license agreement should hold back that territory from a grant of rights. Some companies may even help the artist make a foreign licensing connection through a sub-licensing clause in the agreement.

Term

All licensing agreements should have a term — a fixed period of time for which the license is granted. The term might be as short as two years or as long as the licensee keeps the product in stock. Except for work for hire agreements that acquire the work once and for all time, the artist might agree to a single term, or one with a renewable clause, or even a combination of yearly terms provided certain sales goals are reached. When the term expires, all rights to the work should revert back to the artist.

Without term limits, one unwise agreement would almost certainly be disastrous to the entire licensing program. At least term limits can lessen the effects of a licensing mistake. Even a bad agreement will eventually expire and you can start negotiating all over again!

Payment Options

Flat Fee

Frequently, a single image to be used for a card or book jacket, or a design that will be used for a special promotional product line in the mass market will command a flat fee payment rather than a royalty.

Let's suppose that you have shown a series of paintings to a greeting card company and the product manager says that she would like to use them for cards. She says that she has management orders to pay only flat fees for newly acquired work — no ongoing royalties. How do you respond? Some artists expect the continuous revenue flow of the royalty system and will never agree to a flat fee. For other artists, it depends on the situation. An artist might consider a flat fee arrangement for a short term use of a piece of artwork. Many artists ask for more information before considering a flat fee payment. What will the print run be? What will the retail price be? What are the expected sales quantities? With that information, the artist can compare the potential royalties over the life of the product with an up front flat fee offer. The artist may need to weigh the risk of unearned royalties against the certain payment at hand.

All artists at some times in their lives are grateful for flat fee work. It pays the mortgage, it buys the groceries. It is a guaranteed payment in advance of production, not dependent on royalties to be earned from future sales. Sometimes it can be in your best interests to ask for a flat fee payment. If a manufacturer is introducing a new product category to their business and has no history of sales in that category, you may be better off getting all of your money up front rather than waiting to see how the product performs in the marketplace. Of course, if the product is a runaway best-seller, you won't share in that success through royalties. On the other hand, if it does not live up to expectations, you will not share in the failure. A sample flat fee license agreement is included in the Appendices.

Royalties

A royalty is a payment to the artist (usually a percentage of the manufacturer's receipts, but sometimes a fixed amount) based on the price of the products sold. A fair royalty rate is arrived at through a discussion of the general practices of the industry, an understanding of the company's policies and guidelines and an honest dialogue about each party's expectations. Here is where your prior networking can help you. If other artists like yourself have had ongoing happy relationships with the manufacturer you are negotiating with, you can feel comfortable that you will be offered a fair deal. You don't want to have unrealistic expectations — or accept so little that your work is devalued. Mutual respect makes a solid foundation for a successful royalty agreement. A sample royalty-based license agreement is included in the Appendices to this book.

The Advance

Typically, the manufacturer will make an advance payment against royalties to be earned. This payment should be non-refundable and helps to offset the cost to the artist for time and materials. Additionally, the advance serves as a good faith offering by the manufacturer that confirms his or her obligations and commitment to the project. Without an advance, the artist is essentially agreeing to work on speculation, hoping that the manufacturer will indeed produce the product. Some projects that proceed through negotiation do not actually make it to market. The advance is insurance for the artist against that unfortunate event where few or no royalties are earned. Once a product is produced and sold, the advance will have to be earned back before additional royalties are paid to the artist.

Royalty Rates

Some royalties are calculated as a percentage of a retail price of the product sold (typically in the book publishing business), others as a percentage of a net selling price (the price charged to wholesalers) and still others as a percentage of net receipts (accounting for extra selling discounts and promotions). There is a growing trend toward a net receipts basis, where manufacturers ask their licensors to share in the risks as well as the rewards of a highly competitive selling environment. Occasionally, there is an offer of a fixed sum for each unit sold. It may seem attractive at the time, but the artist should be aware that if the product has a long life in the marketplace, that fixed sum will not keep pace with inflation.

The royalty rate and compensation provisions are often the most hotly debated provisions in the negotiation process. Royalty rates can vary from two to twenty percent and even more, depending on the rate basis, the market, the industry, the category and the value of the work to the company. Any discussion here of typical rates can only be misleading to an artist, because of the many factors that determine fairness.

Guarantees

Some artists can specify a certain minimum of royalty earnings that must be achieved annually for as long as the agreement is in force. Should the sales not earn that sum, the manufacturer must make up the difference each year for the term of the contract. A guarantee may be offered in lieu of an advance or in addition to one. Artists with celebrity status may feel that their exposure in the marketplace requires a guarantee from the manufacturer in order to protect the value of their names.

Details of the License Agreement

The above are the essential points that you will most likely cover in your negotiations. These mutually agreed-upon points will then be translated into a licensing agreement, a binding legal contract that commits you and the manufacturer to its terms. But if it's that simple, why are contracts so long and wordy? The answer is that the rest of the contract covers the details. The details will define how you will work together; what you can expect of each other; what you cannot expect of each other and what your remedies will be if either of you fail each other.

In addition to the specific business terms, all license agreements should include the important "boilerplate" provisions. When things are going well between licensor and licensee (and most of the time they do), neither party concerns itself with the "boilerplate" provisions of the contract. But lawsuits, judgments and penalties arise out of that same boilerplate. You should at least understand each provision's content and intentions and be sure that the agreement fully protects your interests.

Quality of Merchandise; Samples

The license agreement should require the license to manufacture the product in style, appearance and quality to the licensee's own highest standards. This is not to say that it will be to *the artist's* standards. The agreement will require that the licensee submit samples of the finished licensed product and that the quality of all future products be consistent with the submitted sample. Here, also, is where an agreed number of finished samples is specified.

Royalties; Reports and Payments

A procedure for payments and sales reporting should be outlined in the agreement. Negotiation points are the frequency of the reports, the form of payments and whether payment is through an agent or directly to the artist.

Books and Records

The licensee promises to keep accurate records and will let the artist, or a representative of the artist, inspect the books if necessary.

Diligence

In this clause, the licensee agrees to use the best business practices to promote and sell the products. It might not be a bad idea to agree upon what constitutes best efforts on the part of the licensee, in order to avoid problems later on.

Copyrights

In every license agreement, there should be a clear statement of who will own the copyright to the original work, adaptations and modifications. The agreement establishes and confirms ownership of the original material. It also assigns responsibility for registering copyrights and trademarks.

Legal Markings

The licensee should agree to mark all products and packaging with appropriate copyright notices and trademarks to protect the works under universal copyright and trademark laws.

Nature of the Relationship

The agreement should clearly state the relationship between the two parties. In most cases, the agreement will stipulate that the relationship is a license and is not to be construed as anything else, e.g., employee-employer relationship, partnership, joint venture etc.

Representations and Warranties

Both parties warrant that they have the right to form the agreement. Every artist will be asked to make certain representations and warranties to the manufacturer. These reps and warranties include:

- the artist has the right to license the work;
- the work is original;
- the same rights have not been granted to another party for the same products;
- the work is free from any liens or pending lawsuits; and
- the work is not illegal.

Indemnities

The artist may promise that if there are any suits brought against the artist with respect to the works or ownership of the works, the licensee will not be held liable. In return, the licensee promises that if there are any suits or claims arising out of the manufacture of the products, the licensor will not be liable.

Infringements

This clause states who will prosecute known infringers and who will bear the costs of doing so. This clause also stipulates how any sums that are recovered from these law suits will be distributed.

Term and Termination

These provisions outline the procedures and conditions for termination of the agreement. Considerations for renewal and procedures for disposing of finished products after termination are also discussed.

Notices and Statements

This section of the license agreement dictates how and in what form the parties will communicate, i.e., first class mail, registered mail, E-Mail, telephone, etc.

Assignment

Can the licensee assign the agreement to another manufacturer? Most agreements clearly state that this is not an option. This part of the agreement also states that it should be binding on any heirs and successors in the business and accrue to the benefit of the licensor's heirs and survivors.

Jurisdiction

If a situation arises where either party seeks legal remedy, in what court would it be heard? The state where you reside? Where the manufacturer is located? Is arbitration an option for dispute resolution? Several years ago I was involved in a suit where, buried in the boilerplate, was the statement that suits would be tried in another state. Because my attorney did not have a license to practice there, I needed to hire another attorney at considerable expense and discomfort. We finally settled out of court, but the distress of that experience stayed with me. Now I always check the jurisdiction clause. Some licensors suggest that all suits be brought in the state of the party who must defend. This is presumed to discourage frivolous suits. However you resolve this issue, you should be aware that different states' laws can help or hinder your quest for justice and the defense of your actions.

Severability and Integration

These clauses are included in almost every type of license agreement. A severability clause states that if any clause of the contract is invalid, it will not affect the remainder of the agreement. An integration clause provides that the license agreement is the final and entire understanding between the parties and that it incorporates all prior written or oral agreements between the parties.

SEVEN:
Should You Use an Agent?

Soliciting business, negotiating terms, drawing up contracts and overseeing the performance of licensees can be full time work. If you feel that the process is too time-consuming or difficult, you may want to find a licensing agent to represent you.

Advantages of Hiring an Agent

Hiring a license agent to handle the business responsibilities of licensing is an option for many artists. The following are some of the advantages of agent representation.

• Licensing is their full-time work. Licensing agents can devote all of their energy and time to finding licensees for their clients. They have developed a range of professional, person-to-person relationships with the decision makers in the various industries. They have trained and experienced eyes that recognize the commercial potential of an artist's work and in which industry and for what product it might best be exploited.

• An agent speaks on your behalf. This is a powerful advantage. Your agent can speak without embarrassment about your skill and talent. It is impossible to tell someone how wonderful you are without seeming an arrogant fool! Your agent, however, is expected to praise you and your work. The agent can sing your praises and say all those wonderful things that no one could possibly say about oneself without seeming like a pathological egotist. The agent is expected to sell you and your work. It is usually easier to sell someone else than it is to sell one's self.

• Many manufacturers prefer to work through agents. Using an agent allows the manufacturer to freely speak his mind about the property, voice his criticisms and doubts, compare the property with another and negotiate the true value of the artist's work. The agent can then filter this discussion back to the artist in a way that will create a good working relationship between the artist and the licensee. Some manufacturers look to licensing agents to pre-screen properties. Manufacturers come to trust certain agents' sensibilities. They look to agents for advice and design direction. Therefore, they will be predisposed to respect your work to the same degree that they respect the agent's advice.

• An agent can protect your sensitivities and build your confidence. A licensee, in negotiating a royalty rate for a property may say, "Yeah, it's good.

But I've seen better. It's not that good!" If that kind of frank talk about you as an artist upsets you, you would be well advised to find an agent to represent you. Contract negotiations can be a high-stakes game. Money is being committed and all parties want to get the best deal they can. If you can't remove your "creative hat" for a "business hat," you are better off working in your studio and leaving the hurly-burly of the business to an agent.

• An agent will be your watchdog. It is the agent's job to be sure that royalty reports and payments are delivered in a timely manner; that their artists receive correct documentation for income tax purposes; that the licensee complies with quality manufacturing standards as outlined in the contract; that the artist receives the required number of finished sample products and that copyrights and trademarks are protected.

In all areas of the licensing process, the agent is your eyes and ears to be sure that you and your rights are protected. The agent will leave you free to do what you do best: create more art.

Finding an Agent

Finding an agent who is willing to represent you can be almost as difficult as finding a licensee. The analyses and preparations described in the previous chapters should be conducted prior to seeking an agent. You will need to have a firm handle on the type of art you want to create and license and the type of program you envision for your artwork. Then, you need to communicate this to an agent who will be able to go out and structure a program by finding the right licensees. As an artist, you will need to feel comfortable with the agent, because the agent will represent you to the manufacturers that will get your program off the ground.

Once you have determined what your goals are and decided to use an agent, you need to consider how to present yourself and your art to potential agents. You will want to have an attractive presentation to make to the agent and you will want to be able to discuss your work and its potential markets and products. The same rules generally apply as those that should be followed when making a presentation to a manufacturer. Be sure to have a "handle" on your work and be able to capture the essence of your work in a quick and decisive manner. Any materials that you bring as representations of your art should reinforce the theme of your work.

Resources for Finding Agents

The International Licensing Industry Merchandisers' Association (LIMA) is the industry's not-for-profit trade association. Members include licensors, licensing agents and manufacturers. LIMA sponsors an annual international licensing and merchandising exposition in New York City in June. LIMA also publishes *The Licensing Resource Directory: The Who's Who in the Licensing Industry*. You can contact LIMA at 350 Fifth Avenue, Suite 6210, New York, New York. Certainly you should leap at an opportunity to attend the licensing exposition. Agents, manufacturers, artists and designers scout for properties and clients at this show. It is a networker's paradise.

Publications pertinent to the licensing business can inform you about agents and the type of properties they represent. *The Licensing Journal, The Licensing Book. The Licensing Letter, Licensing Today* and *Licensing Trends* are a few that you may want to review. (You may find their addresses in the Appendices.).

Trade publications for markets that are suitable for your work often publish licensing news. Who's representing what art and to whom? Note the names of the agents that are representing artists with which you would feel compatible; the agents who are working with manufacturers that you think would be consistent with your style. A query letter to those agents, explaining your work and your wish to send your portfolio would be appropriate.

Ask manufacturers to recommend agents. Whenever you have the opportunity to discuss your work with a potential licensee, ask about agents.

They may be very fond of one, despise another. They may only work through agents. They may prefer not to. This one-on-one personal information can be far more valuable than a scatter shot approach to finding the right agent for you.

Contacting Potential Agents

A query letter, brief bio and a good representative sample of your work should be your first formal contact. If possible, you can then ask for a meeting so that you can make a full presentation of your portfolio. If distance makes it impossible to meet face to face, you will then want to send your portfolio with slides and transparencies. In this situation, it is advisable to contact the agent first, since to send this valuable material without any contact is very risky.

The Agent Agreement

Once you find an agent who is interested in representing your artwork, you will want to discuss the terms of your agreement. Licensing agents typically expect from twenty-five to fifty percent of the royalties earned on your behalf. So the extent of their interest in you and your work can be somewhat measured by the potential income that you represent.

Like the license agreement, the agent agreement needs to address certain issues. The following is a list of some of the considerations that will have to be negotiated with the agent.

Property and Product Categories

The agent agreement needs to address what artwork will be covered. Will it be only existing art? Or will it include all future works? Likewise, the agreement should state for what product categories the agent can solicit licenses. There are various reasons for limiting the agent's representation in these areas. For example, the artist may have strong contacts in one area of the market, but no exposure in another. In this case, the agreement can be structured so that the agent will look to secure agreements in the unexplored areas, which are specifically delineated in the agreement. Perhaps an agent has a particularly good relationship with a certain manufacturer and the artist only wants to be represented by an agent to that company. In some cases, product categories are restricted by prior licensing agreements. These points need to be addressed before granting representation rights to an agent.

Term

How much time will you grant the agent to try to solicit work for you? You need to give the agent enough time to tell your story and ride out the marketing cycles of the various manufacturers' product categories. How will you deal with renewals and termination?

Commission

Typically, agents will negotiate the license on behalf of the artists, and collect all funds due. They deduct their commission and send the remainder to the artist. The commission is based on the gross royalty earnings from the property licensed. A relatively untried artist will require a greater expenditure of time and effort on the agent's part than a popular artist with a licensing history. Commissions can be negotiated — sometimes with a declining scale as the artist begins to earn more royalties. But the commission is the engine that fuels the agent's work. Sharing even one-half of truly outstanding royalties with your agent can be far better for you than to keep all of a few meager earnings for yourself.

The Artist/Agent Relationship

Understanding the role of an agent so that the agent can work on your behalf is essential for a healthy artist/agent relationship. It takes confidence in your agent's experience and judgment to be able to accept his or her critique of your work.

It requires respect for the agent's professional role in the industry to let him represent you. Don't get in the way. Let your agent be the contact. Let your agent tell the story. Let your agent manage the selling strategy. Let your agent negotiate. Let your agent do the job.

Patience is essential. Like a good marriage, a good artist/agent relationship takes time to develop. Trust is forged out of experience, achieving common goals and sharing the rewards. In time, with the right agent, you can attain that.

EIGHT:
A Word From the Lawyers — Protecting the Artwork[1]

Artists have a unique advantage over virtually every other type of creative individual when it comes to protecting their properties. While inventors and designers are faced with the enormous costs of seeking and maintaining patent protection for their designs and inventions, the copyright laws were initiated with the artist and author in mind. Of all the forms of intellectual property protection, copyright protection is, by far, the least expensive and easiest to obtain. The filing fees with the Copyright Office are modest and there is no need to retain an attorney to file the copyright application. The form is that easy!

Some artists also look to the trademark laws to protect their names and signatures in much the same manner as Pierre Cardin or Halston.

---

[1] The author would like to express her appreciation to Gregory J. Battersby of Grimes & Battersby in Stamford, Connecticut, for his assistance in the preparation of this chapter.

Trademark protection is available for the name in block form as well as the actual signature.

Some forms of sculpture may even qualify for design patent protection. To place these forms of protection in their proper context, the following is an overview of the intellectual property laws as they apply to the creation and licensing of artwork.

Forms of Protection

In general, there is a great deal of confusion as to the differences between patent, trademark and copyright protection. Intellectual property attorneys are frequently asked by new clients to "patent" a new product name. Anyone familiar with intellectual property rights knows that one patents an invention and obtains a trademark for a name.

The problem (or luxury) facing the intellectual property attorney is that oftentimes a property can be protected under a variety of different legal theories. For example, a three-dimensional object (for example, a lamp) can be protected by a utility patent (covering the unique manner of attachment of the stem to the base), by a design patent (covering the aesthetic appearance of the lamp), by a copyright (covering the original drawings of the lamp and the lamp as a derivative work), or even by a trademark registration (covering the unique appearance of the lamp which the public has come to associate exclusively with a particular manufacturer).

With the exception of copyright protection, all other forms of protection are territorial in nature. That means that a United States trademark registration or patent will only protect the property within the boundaries of the United States. Separate registrations or patents must be filed on a country by country basis to protect properties abroad. Due to a number of international conventions to which the United States is a signatory, however, copyright protection is international in scope. Thus, a valid copyright registration in the United States will protect the creator from infringement in virtually every other country in the world.

Patent Protection

Generally speaking, utility and design patents are relied upon to protect, respectively, the functional and aesthetic aspects of an invention;[2] copy-

---

[2] See generally Borchard, A Trademark Is Not a Patent or a Copyright, United States Trademark Association (1990); and McCarthy, TRADEMARKS AND UNFAIR COMPETITION, §6.1-6.9. A number of excellent treatises have been written on the subjects of patent, trademark and copyright law and this text will not attempt to duplicate their generally thorough treatment of those subjects. This text will, instead, attempt to present a general overview of the subject of intellectual property law with particular emphasis on how the various forms of protection can be effectively used to protect merchandising properties.

rights are relied upon to protect literary works, musical works, dramatic works, choreographic works, pictorial, graphic, and sculptural works, and sound recordings;[3] and trademarks are relied upon to protect words, names, designs and three-dimensional shapes that function as indicators of commercial source, origin, or sponsorship.[4]

Artists will rarely, if ever, look to the utility patent laws to protect their works. Aesthetic works simply do not qualify for patent protection, because there must be some element of functionality. As such, utility patent protection is generally not available for the artist.

Design patent protection is, however, a horse of a different color. Design patents are commonly used to protect three-dimensional objects which could include works such as sculptures, dolls and the like. Where the resultant piece of art takes a three-dimensional shape, design patent protection is potentially available.

One obtains design patent protection by filing an application with the United States Patent and Trademark Office (PTO) in Washington, DC. As of the writing of this book, the Patent and Trademark Office filing fee for a design patent application was $155 for a small entity and $310 for a regular entity. Generally speaking, it is advisable to retain

---

[3] See 35 U.S.C. § 1 et seq.
[4] See 17 U.S.C. § 101 et seq.

the services of a patent attorney to prepare and prosecute the patent application. Thus, between PTO fees and attorney fees, you should expect the total cost for a design patent to be between $1,000-$2,000, depending upon whether there are any problems encountered during prosecution.

While there has been a tremendous improvement in recent years in the responsiveness of the Patent and Trademark Office, you should expect that it will take between one and two years before the design patent issues. Design patents are valid for fourteen years from the date of issuance, and you will have no rights in the creation unless and until a patent issues from the PTO. Simply stated, that means that you will not be able to sue another for infringement unless the patent issues, and then only for sales commencing with the date of issuance.

Trademark Protection

In contrast, trademarks are used to protect names, words, logos and the like that serve as indicators of source, origin or sponsorship. We all know the COCA-COLA trademark, which serves to identify a particular brand of soft drink from the competition. Trademark protection has also now extended to such diverse forms of indicators as product shapes (the Mogan David wine bottle), colors (pink for fiberglass insulation), character images ("Snoopy on a Doghouse") and logos (the Nike "swoosh" stripe).

In the art community, trademark protection is used in a number of different ways. Many artists have registered their names as trademarks in much the same fashion that Pierre Cardin or Halston registered and licensed their names. Clearly, when the name of an artist actually appears on a product, that name serves a classic trademark function and is protectable under the trademark laws. The more prominent the name, the greater the trademark rights and licensing potential.

Artists and manufacturers frequently use names to identify their particular collections, e.g., The Sunset Collection. Such a collection name can and does serve as an indication of source and, as such, is protectable under the trademark laws. Many manufacturers choose not to register these collection names, however, due to the fact that they change so frequently. Where, however, a particular name is used over a period of time, it might be wise to seek appropriate trademark protection for the name.

Artwork applied to a product can also serve as a trademark. The artwork depicting Snoopy sitting on his doghouse, when applied to the front of a shirt or mug, serves as an indicator of source, origin or sponsorship. Thus, it functions in a trademark sense and has been registered as such.

Trademark rights in the United States are based on use, not registration. That differs from other countries where trademark rights are based almost exclusively on registration. In such countries, the one who wins the race to the local patent and trademark office usually comes away with the trademark. In the United States, however, the first to use a mark in interstate commerce on a particular product or service will typically have superior rights to second-comers.

Since trademark rights are use-based in the United States, the product or service on which the mark is used is highly relevant. Trademarks are classified into 42 different classes depending upon the product or service. You can obtain rights for a particular mark in one class while another may have rights for that same mark in another class. Consider for example, Paramount chicken and Paramount Pictures for motion pictures. Then, of course, there is Paramount movers. The test applied by courts and the Patent and Trademark Office is whether there would be any likelihood of confusion between the two uses. If you would not associate Cadillac dogfood with General Motors and its line of automobiles, there is no likelihood of confusion and, as such, the pet food manufacturer can adopt and use the name.

While trademark rights are created upon the commencement of use, it is always wise to register the mark with the United States Patent and

Trademark Office where there is use in interstate commerce. You can also obtain appropriate state trademark registrations for marks that are used on an intrastate basis. Registration of a mark serves as notice to the public that you consider yourself to be the owner of such mark and is a deterrent to adoption and use by others. More-over, registration offers numerous procedural ad-vantages in litigation when attempting to sue in-fringers.

An application to register a mark with the United States Patent and Trademark Office can be filed based on either actual use of the mark in commerce or on a bona fide intention to use the mark in commerce. No registration will issue un-less actual use is effected, however. The current PTO fee for filing a trademark application is $245 per class. The cost of filing and prosecuting a trade-mark application through an attorney with nor-mal prosecution will typically be in the $1000 range for a single class application. From start to finish, you can expect that the application process will take at least a year before any registration issues. Unlike the case with patent protection, however, the owner of an unregistered trademark can bring an action against an infringer under state com-mon law or under the false designation of origin section of the Lanham Act.

The term of a federal trademark registration is ten years. Use must be demonstrated during the fifth and sixth year of the first term in order to maintain the registration. Trademark registrations may be renewed for additional ten year terms provided that use of the trademark continues. There are some trademark registrations that have been on the Principal Register at the PTO for well over a hundred years and are stronger now than they ever have been. It should be noted that a trademark registration for a mark that is not being used is subject to attack and cancellation.

Copyright Protection

Far and away, the most common form of protection for artwork is copyright protection under the Copyright Act. Copyright protection finds its genesis in the United States Constitution and covers any work of authorship fixed in a tangible medium of expression, now known or later developed, from which it can be perceived, reproduced or otherwise communicated, either directly or with the aid of a machine.

Works of authorship for copyright purposes include the following categories:
(1) literary works;
(2) musical works, including any accompanying words;
(3) dramatic works, including any accompanying music;
(4) pantomimes and choreographic works;

(5) pictorial, graphic and sculptural works;

(6) motion pictures and other audiovisual works;

(7) sound recordings;

(8) architectural works.

From the perspective of the artist, the most significant category of works of authorship is "pictorial, graphic, and sculptural works" which the Copyright Act defines as including:

> two-dimensional and three-dimensional works of fine, graphic, and applied art, photographs, prints and art reproductions, maps, globes, charts, diagrams, models and technical drawings, including architectural plans. Such works shall include works of artistic craftsmanship insofar as their form but not their mechanical or utilitarian aspects are concerned....

Virtually all artwork is subject to copyright protection, provided that it is "original." The owner of a copyrighted work, according to the Copyright Act, has the right: (1) to reproduced the copyrighted works in copies or phonorecords; (2) to prepare derivative works based upon the copyrighted work; (3) to distribute copies or phonorecords of the copyrighted work to the public by sale or other transfer of ownership, or by rental, lease, or lending; (4) in the case of literary, musical, dramatic, and choreographic works, pantomimes, and motion pictures and other audiovisual works, to perform the copyrighted work publicly; and (5) in the case of literary, musical, dramatic and choreographic works, pantomimes, and pictorial, graphic, or sculptural works, including the individual images of a motion picture or other audio visual work, to display the copyrighted work publicly.

Copyright rights automatically begin at the moment of creation, not when the Copyright Office registers the copyright. Registration of a copyright claim with the Copyright Office is a prerequisite to commencing an infringement action. A delay in actually registering a copyright claim may prevent the copyright owner from seeking statutory damages and recovering attorneys' fees in a litigation. As such, it is wise for you to register your copyright claim at any early date.

Registering a copyright claim with the United States Copyright Office is very simple. For works of art, a form VA is used and the instructions on the form are excellent. A sample of the form VA copyright application is contained in the Appendices. The current filing fee for a copyright application is $20 and it takes between three and four months for the Copyright Office to act on and register the claim. This time period can be accelerated to a matter of a couple of weeks by paying a surcharge to expedite the application. The current fee for an expedited application is $400.

Copyright applications are very simple to complete and the services of an attorney are not required. Many authors and artists regularly fill out and file their own copyright applications.

Copyright rights vest with the creator of the copyrightable material unless the creator is an employee of a company and performed such work as part of his or her position or, alternatively, where the creator is specifically retained as a contractor to create such work. In the latter case, the agreement must specifically recite that any work performed under the agreement is to be deemed a work made for hire and is thus owned by the company. Failure to address this issue may result in the creator retaining the copyright rights in the work even though he or she may have been paid to perform such work.

For works created after January 1, 1978, the term of copyright protection is the life of the author plus fifty years. Works made for hire have a term of seventy-five years from the year of first publication or 100 years from the date of creation, whichever expires first.

Overlapping Protection

It is not uncommon to obtain both trademark and copyright protection for the same work of art, with the copyright protecting its creative or artistic aspect and the trademark protecting it as an indicator of source, origin or sponsorship of the product on which the artwork is applied. By way of example, consider the artistic rendering of SNOOPY sitting on his doghouse basking in the noonday sun. The artistic rendering or drawing is generally protectable under the copyright laws. When that same rendering is incorporated into a decal and applied to the front of a T-shirt, it is protectable as a trademark, since it serves to indicate that the source of the image on the T-shirt is United Feature Syndicate, the owner of the licensing and merchandising rights to the SNOOPY property.

In *Frederick Warne & Co. v. Book Sales, Inc.*,[5] the court recognized the validity of dual protection under the trademark and copyright statutes, stating:

> Dual protection under copyright and trademark laws is particularly appropriate for graphic representations of characters. A character is deemed an artistic creation deserving copyright protection . . .

---

[5] 481 F. Supp. 1191, 1195, 1196, 205 USPQ 444, 449 (S.D.N.Y. 1979). See also *Universal Studios, Inc. v. J.A.R. Sales, Inc.*, 216 USPQ 679 (C.D. Cal. 1982); *Camp Beverly Hills, Inc. v. Camp Cent. Park, Inc.*, 217 USPQ 783 (S.D.N.Y. 1982); *Planters Nut & Chocolate Co. v. Crown Nut Co.*, 305 F.2d 916, 134 USPQ 504 (C.C.P.A. 1962); *Edgar Rice Burroughs, Inc. v. Mann Theaters*, 195 USPQ 159 (C.D. Cal. 1976).

> [it] may also serve to identify the creator, thus meriting protection under theories of trademark or unfair competition . . . . Indeed, because of their special value in distinguishing goods and services, names and pictorial representations of characters are often registered as trademarks under the Lanham Act.

It is important to note the differences between the copyright and trademark statutes. Copyright protection is limited to a term of life of the author plus 50 years for individuals and a term of 75 years from the first publication (or 100 years from creation, whichever expires first) for works made for hire by employees. In contrast, the initial term for a trademark registration is ten years and it may be renewed for like terms as long as the mark is in use. The *Frederick Warne* court viewed this difference in trademark and copyright statutes in the following manner:

> The fact that a copyrightable character or design has fallen into the public domain should not preclude protection under the trademark laws so long as it is shown to have acquired independent trademark significance, identifying in some way the source or sponsorship of the goods. See *Wyatt Earp Enterprises v. Sackman, Inc.,*

157 F. Supp. 621, 116 USPQ 122 (S.D.N.Y. 1958). Because the nature of the property right conferred by copyright is significantly different from that of trademark, trademark protection should be able to co-exist, and possibly overlap, with copyright protection without posing preemption difficulties.

Legal Marking Requirements

The use of appropriate legal notices is very important. Valuable property rights and the ability to collect damages may be lost as a result of failure to comply with the requisite statutory notice provisions. The basic legal notices are the two trademark notices (™ and ®), the copyright notice (©), and the patent notice. The ™ symbol is used to designate a property that is considered a trademark by the owner but is not federally registered. The ® symbol is used to designate a federally registered trademark. The formal copyright notice requires the word "Copyright," the abbreviation "Copr.," or a © followed by the name of the copyright owner and the year of the work's first publication.

Goods that are covered by a pending patent application should be marked "Patent Pending." Upon issuance of a patent, the "Patent Pending" notice should be replaced with a notice identifying the actual patent number, for example, "Patent No. 1,234,567."

Other notices that should be used include the legend "All Rights Reserved," which should follow the standard copyright notice. Use of this designation is particularly important when distribution is contemplated in South American countries.[6] Many countries, including Canada, require products to bear a notice identifying the owner of the property and stating that the product is being manufactured by the licensee under license from the owner. The property owner should be aware of such requirements and make sure that such local laws are being complied with.

---

[6] Article 3 of the Buenos Aires Copyright Convention requires that a statement should appear in the work which indicates the reservation of the property right. Included among the signatories of the Buenos Aires Convention are the United States, Argentina, Brazil, Chile, Colombia, Costa Rica, Cuba, Dominican Republic, Ecuador, Guatemala, Haiti, Honduras, Mexico, Nicaragua, Panama, Paraguay, Peru, Salvador, Uruguay, and Venezuela.

Resources for the Artist

1. Associations

Graphic Artists Guild
11 West 20th Street
New York, NY 10011
Telephone (212) 463-7730

Licensing Industry Merchandisers' Association
("LIMA")
Suite 6210, 350 Fifth Avenue
New York, NY 10118-0110
Telephone: (212) 244-1944

National Association of Artists' Organizations
(NAAO)
918 F Street, N.W., Suite 611
Washington, DC 20004
Telephone: (202) 347-6350

2. Books

THE CREATIVE GUIDE SERIES, Rockport Publishers,
146 Granite Street, Rockport, MA 01966

GRAPHIC ARTISTS GUILD HANDBOOK: PRICING & ETHICAL
GUIDELINES, Graphic Artists Guild, Inc., New
York, NY

ORGANIZING ARTISTS, National Association of Artists' Organizations, Washington, DC

3. Periodicals

Apparel Merchandising
425 Park Avenue
New York, NY 10022
Telephone: (212) 756-5134

Art Business News
777 Summer Street
Stamford, CT 06901

Gift & Stationery Business
1515 Broadway
New York, NY 10036
Telephone: (212) 869-1300

Gifts and Tablewares
1450 Don Mills Road
Don Mills, Ontario, Canada
Telephone: (416) 442-2042

Gifts & Decorative Accessories
51 Madison Avenue
New York, NY 10010
Telephone: (212) 689-4411

Giftware News
P.O. Box 5398
112 Adrossan Court
Deptford, NJ 08096
Telephone: (609) 227-0798

Greetings Magazine
    309 Fifth Avenue
    New York, NY 10016
    Telephone: (212) 594-0880

Home Furnishings Directory
    7 West 34th Street
    New York, NY 10001

Home Textiles Today
    245 West 17th Street
    New York, NY 10011
    Telephone: (212) 337-6906

The Licensing Book
    1501 Broadway, Suite 500
    New York, NY 10036
    Telephone: (212) 575-4510

The Licensing Journal
    P.O. Box 1169
    Stamford, CT 06904-1169
    Telephone: (203) 358-0848

The Licensing Letter
    533 Eighth Street
    Brooklyn, NY 11215
    Telephone: (718) 499-3236

Licensing Trends
    51 Madison Avenue
    New York, NY 10010

Party & Paper
   70 New Canaan Avenue
   Norwalk, CT 06850
   Telephone: (203) 845-8020

Women's Wear Daily
   7 West 34th Street
   New York, NY 10001
   Telephone: (212) 630-3525

4. Trade Shows — A Representative Calendar

January
   – Washington Gift Show, Capital Expo Center, Chantilly, VA
   – New York International Gift Fair, Javits Convention Center, New York, NY
   – International Housewares Show, Chicago, IL
   – Gift Show, World Congress Center, Atlanta, GA
   – Gift Show, Convention Center, Dallas, TX
   – Gift Show, Convention Center, Los Angeles, CA

February
   – San Francisco International Gift Fair, Moscone Center, San Francisco, CA
   – American International Toy Fair, Javits Center, New York, NY

March
   – Boston Gift Show, Bayside Exposition Center, Boston, MA

April
   – New York Home Textiles Show, Javits Convention Center, New York, NY

May
– National Stationery Show, Javits Center, New York, NY

June
– The International Licensing Expo, Javits Convention Center, New York, NY
– SURTEX (Surface Designers) Javits Convention Center, New York, NY

July
– Washington Gift Show, Capital Expo Center, Chantilly, VA
– San Francisco International Gift Fair, Moscone Center, San Francisco, CA
– Gift Show, McCormick Place, Chicago, IL
– Gift Show, World Congress Center, Atlanta, GA

August
– International Gift Fair, Javits Center, New York, NY
– Just Kidstuff & The Museum Source, Javits Center, New York, NY

September
– Boston Gift Show, Bayside Exposition Center, Boston, MA
– National Merchandise Show, Javits Center, New York, NY

October
– New York Home Textiles Show, Javits Center, New York, NY
– International Juvenile Product Show, Dallas Market Hall, Dallas, TX
– National Premium Incentive Show, McCormick Place, Chicago, IL

November
– School and Home Office Products (SHOPA), Dallas Convention Center, Dallas, TX

For a full list of all U.S. Trade Shows: 1996 Tradeshow Week Data Book, 1-800-521-8110

Copyright Application
Form VA (Visual Arts)

FORM VA ■
For a Work of the Visual Arts
UNITED STATES COPYRIGHT OFFICE

REGISTRATION NUMBER

VA   VAU
EFFECTIVE DATE OF REGISTRATION

Month   Day   Year

DO NOT WRITE ABOVE THIS LINE. IF YOU NEED MORE SPACE, USE A SEPARATE CONTINUATION SHEET.

1

TITLE OF THIS WORK ▼   NATURE OF THIS WORK ▼ See instructions

PREVIOUS OR ALTERNATIVE TITLES ▼

PUBLICATION AS A CONTRIBUTION If this work was published as a contribution to a periodical, serial, or collection, give information about the collective work in which the contribution appeared.   Title of Collective Work ▼

If published in a periodical or serial give: Volume ▼   Number ▼   Issue Date ▼   On Pages ▼

2 a

NAME OF AUTHOR ▼   DATES OF BIRTH AND DEATH
                                                          Year Born ▼   Year Died ▼

Was this contribution to the work a   AUTHOR'S NATIONALITY OR DOMICILE   WAS THIS AUTHOR'S CONTRIBUTION TO
"work made for hire"?   Name of Country   THE WORK   If the answer to either
□ Yes   OR { Citizen of ▶_____   Anonymous? □ Yes □ No   of these questions is
□ No   { Domiciled in▶_____   Pseudonymous? □ Yes □ No   "Yes," see detailed instructions.

NOTE

Under the law, the "author" of a "work made for hire" is generally the employer, not the employee (see instructions). For any part of this work that was "made for hire" check "Yes" in the space provided, give the employer (or other person for whom the work was prepared) as "Author" of that part, and leave the space for dates of birth and death blank.

NATURE OF AUTHORSHIP Check appropriate box(es). See instructions
□ 3-Dimensional sculpture   □ Map   □ Technical drawing
□ 2-Dimensional artwork   □ Photograph   □ Text
□ Reproduction of work of art □ Jewelry design □ Architectural work
□ Design on sheetlike material

b

NAME OF AUTHOR ▼   DATES OF BIRTH AND DEATH
                                                          Year Born ▼   Year Died ▼

Was this contribution to the work a   AUTHOR'S NATIONALITY OR DOMICILE   WAS THIS AUTHOR'S CONTRIBUTION TO
"work made for hire"?   Name of Country   THE WORK   If the answer to either
□ Yes   OR { Citizen of ▶_____   Anonymous? □ Yes □ No   of these questions is
□ No   { Domiciled in▶_____   Pseudonymous? □ Yes □ No   "Yes," see detailed instructions.

NATURE OF AUTHORSHIP Check appropriate box(es). See instructions
□ 3-Dimensional sculpture   □ Map   □ Technical drawing
□ 2-Dimensional artwork   □ Photograph   □ Text
□ Reproduction of work of art □ Jewelry design □ Architectural work
□ Design on sheetlike material

3 a

YEAR IN WHICH CREATION OF THIS
WORK WAS COMPLETED This information   b Complete this information Month▶ _____ Day▶ _____ Year▶ _____
◀Year must be given in all cases.   ONLY if this work has been published.   ◀ Nation

DATE AND NATION OF FIRST PUBLICATION OF THIS PARTICULAR WORK

4

See instructions before completing this space.

COPYRIGHT CLAIMANT(S) Name and address must be given even if the claimant is the same as the author given in space 2. ▼

TRANSFER If the claimant(s) named here in space 4 is (are) different from the author(s) named in space 2, give a brief statement of how the claimant(s) obtained ownership of the copyright. ▼

APPLICATION RECEIVED

ONE DEPOSIT RECEIVED

TWO DEPOSITS RECEIVED

FUNDS RECEIVED

DO NOT WRITE HERE / OFFICE USE ONLY

MORE ON BACK ▶ · Complete all applicable spaces (numbers 5-9) on the reverse side of this page.
                · See detailed instructions.   · Sign the form at line 8.

DO NOT WRITE HERE
Page 1 of _____ pages

EXAMINED BY	FORM VA
CHECKED BY	
☐ CORRESPONDENCE Yes	FOR COPYRIGHT OFFICE USE ONLY

DO NOT WRITE ABOVE THIS LINE. IF YOU NEED MORE SPACE, USE A SEPARATE CONTINUATION SHEET.

PREVIOUS REGISTRATION Has registration for this work, or for an earlier version of this work, already been made in the Copyright Office?
☐ Yes ☐ No If your answer is "Yes," why is another registration being sought? (Check appropriate box) ▼
a. ☐ This is the first published edition of a work previously registered in unpublished form.
b. ☐ This is the first application submitted by this author as copyright claimant.
c. ☐ This is a changed version of the work, as shown by space 6 on this application.
If your answer is "Yes," give: **Previous Registration Number ▼**   **Year of Registration ▼**

5

DERIVATIVE WORK OR COMPILATION Complete both space 6a and 6b for a derivative work; complete only 6b for a compilation.
a. **Preexisting Material** Identify any preexisting work or works that this work is based on or incorporates. ▼

b. **Material Added to This Work** Give a brief, general statement of the material that has been added to this work and in which copyright is claimed. ▼

6

See instructions
before completing
this space.

DEPOSIT ACCOUNT If the registration fee is to be charged to a Deposit Account established in the Copyright Office, give name and number of Account.
Name ▼   **Account Number ▼**

7

CORRESPONDENCE Give name and address to which correspondence about this application should be sent. Name/Address/Apt/City/State/ZIP ▼

Area Code and Telephone Number ►

Be sure to
give your
daytime phone
◄ number

CERTIFICATION* I, the undersigned, hereby certify that I am the
check only one ▼
☐ author
☐ other copyright claimant
☐ owner of exclusive right(s)
☐ authorized agent of _____
    Name of author or other copyright claimant, or owner of exclusive right(s) ▲

of the work identified in this application and that the statements made
by me in this application are correct to the best of my knowledge.

Typed or printed name and date ▼ If this application gives a date of publication in space 3, do not sign and submit it before that date.
              Date►

☞ Handwritten signature (X) ▼

8

MAIL CERTIFI- CATE TO	Name ▼	YOU MUST • Complete all necessary spaces • Sign your application in space 8	**9**
		SEND ALL 3 ELEMENTS IN THE SAME PACKAGE	
Certificate will be mailed in window envelope	Number/Street/Apt ▼	1. Application form 2. Nonrefundable $20 filing fee in check or money order payable to Register of Copyrights 3. Deposit material	The Copyright Office has the authority to set just fees at 5-year inter- vals, based on changes in the Consumer Price Index. The next adjust-
	City/State/ZIP ▼	MAIL TO Register of Copyrights Library of Congress Washington, D.C. 20559-6000	ment is due in 1996. Please contact the Copyright Office after July 1995 to determine the actual fee schedule.

*17 U.S.C. § 506(e): Any person who knowingly makes a false representation of a material fact in the application for copyright registration provided for by section 409, or in any written statement filed in connection with the application, shall be fined not more than $2,500.

July 1993—300,000   ⊛ PRINTED ON RECYCLED PAPER   ⁎U.S. GOVERNMENT PRINTING OFFICE: 1993-342-582/80,021

APPENDIX THREE:

Sample Work For Hire
Short-Form Agreement, Flat Fee

THIS AGREEMENT is made this _____ day of
_____, 199 _____, by and between
_____, a _____
corporation with offices at _____
("MANUFACTURER") and _____
_____, whose address is _____
_____ ("ARTIST") under which ARTIST agrees
to produce the work product specified below under the following terms and conditions:

(1)   ARTIST agrees to produce the following
work product: _____
_____
(2)   Compensation (e.g., hourly rate, project
rate, etc.):_____
(3)   Deadline: _____
(4)   Additional Requirements: _____
_____

(5)   ARTIST agrees to produce the work product described in (1) in accordance with the requirements set forth in (4) by the deadline set in (3).
Time is of the essence and ARTIST, therefore,
agrees that ARTIST's compensation shall be contingent upon the timely completion of the work

product to MANUFACTURER's satisfaction by the deadline set in (3).

(6)   Unless otherwise provided in (2), MANU-FACTURER agrees to pay ARTIST the compensation set forth in (2) within thirty days after the deadline set in (3) provided that the ARTIST has turned the work product over to MANUFACTURER, completed to MANUFACTURER's satisfaction, by the deadline.

(7)   The work product shall be a Work for Hire (as such are defined under the U.S. Copyright Laws) owned by and for the benefit of MANUFAC-TURER and if it does not qualify as a Work for Hire, ARTIST will and hereby does assign to MANU-FACTURER all of his/her right, title and interest in the work product, including all copyrights, patents, trademarks and other proprietary rights. The Work for Hire Agreement between MANUFAC-TURER and ARTIST is hereby incorporated herein by reference.

MANUFACTURER   **ARTIST**

By:_____   By:_____
Title:_____   Title:_____
Date:_____   Date:_____

Sample Work For Hire
Long-Form Agreement, Flat Fee

THIS AGREEMENT is made this _____ day of
_____, 199_____ by and between
_____, a _____
corporation with offices at _____
_____ ("MANUFACTURER") and _____
_____, whose address is
_____ ("ARTIST") un-
der which ARTIST agrees to produce the work product specified below under the following terms and
conditions:

(1)   ARTIST agrees to produce the following
work product: _____

_____

(2)   Compensation (e.g., hourly rate, project
rate, etc.): _____

_____

(3)   Deadline: _____
(4)   Additional Requirements: _____

_____

(5)   ARTIST agrees to produce the work product described in (1) in accordance with the requirements set forth in (4) by the deadline set in (3).

Time is of the essence and ARTIST, therefore, agrees that ARTIST's compensation shall be contingent upon the timely completion of the work product to MANUFACTURER's satisfaction by the deadline set in (3). After delivery of the completed work product, ARTIST shall make any revisions to the work product requested by MANUFACTURER within the time specified by MANUFACTURER for such revisions.

(6)   Unless otherwise provided in (2), MANUFACTURER agrees to pay ARTIST the compensation set forth in (2) within _____ (___) days after the deadline set in (3) provided that the ARTIST has turned the work product over to MANUFACTURER, completed to MANUFACTURER's satisfaction, by the deadline, or in the event revisions are requested, when those revisions have been completed to MANUFACTURER's satisfaction.

(7)   The work product shall be a Work for Hire (as such are defined under the U.S. Copyright Laws) owned by and for the benefit of MANUFACTURER and if it does not qualify as a Work for Hire, ARTIST will and hereby does assign to MANUFACTURER all of his/her right, title and interest in the work product, including all copyrights, patents, trademarks and other proprietary rights.

(A)   Upon request, ARTIST will take such steps as are necessary to enable MANUFACTURER to record such assignment, at MANUFACTURER's expense.

(B)   ARTIST will sign, upon request, any documents needed to confirm that the work product is a Work for Hire and/or to effectuate the assignment of his/her rights therein to MANUFACTURER. ARTIST further agrees to assist MANUFACTURER and its agents, upon request, in preparing U.S. and foreign copyright, trademark and/or patent applications covering the work product and will sign any such applications, upon request, and deliver them to MANUFACTURER.

(8)   It is understood and agreed that MANUFACTURER has the right to use or not use the work product and to use, reproduce, re-use, alter, modify, edit or change the work product as it sees fit and for any purpose and that the work product shall not be returned.

(9)   ARTIST shall have no right, title or interest in the work product, nor any license to use, sell, exploit, copy or further develop such work product.

(10) ARTIST's agreed-to compensation on an hourly or per-project basis will be full payment for any work product ARTIST generates and ARTIST will not be entitled to any royalties or proceeds received by MANUFACTURER from the commercialization in any manner of the work product or project.

(11) ARTIST represents and warrants that the work product shall be original, and shall not infringe upon the rights of any other person or party.

In the event of a breach of this representation and warranty, ARTIST shall immediately return to MANUFACTURER all monies received under this Agreement and shall be liable for any consequential damages resulting therefrom.

(12) This Agreement will be binding upon and inure to the benefit of MANUFACTURER, its successors and assigns and ARTIST, his/her successors and assigns, heirs, executors, administrators and/or other legal representatives.

(13) This Agreement shall be governed by the laws of New York.

MANUFACTURER

By: _____
Print Name: _____
Title: _____
Date: _____

ARTIST

By: _____
Print Name: _____
Title: _____
Date: _____

Sample Work for Hire Agreement
Royalty-Based

THIS AGREEMENT is made this _____ day of _____, 199 _____ by and between _____ _____, a _____ cor-poration with offices at _____ _____ ("MANUFACTURER") and _____ with offices at _____ ("ARTIST").

WHEREAS, MANUFACTURER desires to retain the services of the ARTIST on a project by project basis as identified in Schedule A attached hereto (the "Projects") to provide artwork to MANUFAC-TURER for use on certain of its products.

WHEREAS, ARTIST is willing and able to provide such art services to MANUFACTURER in accordance with the terms recited herein.

NOW, THEREFORE, in consideration of the premises and of the mutual promises and covenants herein contained, the parties hereto agree as follows:

1. Retention and Duties of Artist

(A)   MANUFACTURER hereby retains the services of ARTIST to provide certain art related services for MANUFACTURER in connection with the Projects, including ideas, artwork, designs, plans, documents, concepts, inventions, devices, samples, prototypes and improvements (hereinafter called the "Work Product").

(B)   ARTIST is an independent contractor and not an employee of MANUFACTURER. Unless otherwise expressly agreed to in writing, ARTIST shall not be entitled to or eligible for any benefits or programs otherwise given by MANUFACTURER to its employees.

2. Compensation of Artist

(A)   In consideration for the services performed by the ARTIST as promised hereunder, MANUFACTURER agrees to pay to ARTIST the royalty recited in Schedule A (the "Royalty") based on MANUFACTURER's Net Sales of project-related products incorporating the Work Product ("Project Products").

(B)   The Royalty owed ARTIST shall be calculated on a quarterly calendar basis (the "Royalty Period") and shall be payable no later than thirty (30) days after the termination of the preceding full calendar quarter, i.e., commencing on the first 91st) day of January, April, July and October, except that the first and last calendar quarters may be "short" depending on the effective date of this Agreement.

(C) For each Royalty Period, MANUFAC-TURER shall provide ARTIST with a written royalty statement reciting, on a design-by-design basis, the number of units sold, quantity shipped, gross invoice, amount billed customers less discounts, allowances and returns.

(D) "Net Sales" shall mean MANUFACT-URER's gross sales (the gross invoice amount billed customers) of Project Products, less discounts and allowances actually shown on the invoices and, further, less any bona fide returns (net of all returns actually made or allowed as supported by credit memoranda actually issued to the customers) up to the amount of the actual sales of the Project Products during the Royalty Period.

(E) MANUFACTURER's obligations for the payment of Royalties shall survive expiration or termination of this Agreement and will continue for so long as MANUFACTURER continues to sell the Project Products.

3. Ownership and Use of Artwork

(A) MANUFACTURER owns all rights to all past, pending and future Projects and all Work Product relating thereto, including copyrights, patents, trademarks, inventions and other proprietary rights. All work of the ARTIST on the Projects and all Work Product generated in connection therewith is and shall be considered as Works for Hire (as such are defined under the U.S. Copyright Laws) and, as such, such Work Product shall be owned by and for the benefit of MANUFACTURER.

(B)   MANUFACTURER has the right to use or not use the Work Product and to use, reproduce, re-use, alter, modify, edit or change the Work Products as it sees fit and for any purpose.

(C)   ARTIST shall have no right, title or interest in any past, pending or future Project or Work Product, nor any license to use, sell, exploit, copy or further develop any such Project or Work Product.

(D)   In the event that it should be determined that any of such Work Product does not qualify as a Work for Hire, ARTIST will and hereby does assign to MANUFACTURER all right, title and interest which it may possess in such Work Product including, but not limited to, all copyright and proprietary rights relating thereto. Upon request, ARTIST will take such steps as are necessary to enable MANUFACTURER to record such assignment, at MANUFACTURER's expense.

4. Intellectual Property Protection

(A)   ARTIST will sign, upon request, any documents needed to confirm that any specific Work Product or Project is a Work for Hire and/or to effectuate the assignment of his/her rights therein to MANUFACTURER.

(B)   ARTIST will assist MANUFACTURER and its agents, upon request, in preparing U.S. and foreign copyright, trademark and/or patent applications covering the Projects and/or Work Product. ARTIST will sign any such applications, upon request, and deliver them to MANUFACTURER. MANUFACTURER will bear all expenses which it causes to be incurred in connection with such copyright, trademark and/or patent protection.

5. Non-Disclosure

(A)   It is recognized that during the course of his employment with MANUFACTURER, ARTIST may have occasion to conceive, create, develop, review or receive information which is considered by MANUFACTURER to be confidential or proprietary, including information relating to inventions, patent, trademark and copyright applications, improvements, know-how, specifications, drawings, cost data, process flow diagrams, customer and supplier lists, bills, ideas and/or any other written material referring to same (the "Confidential Information"). Both during the term of his employment and thereafter:

1.   ARTIST agrees to maintain in confidence such Confidential Information unless or until: (a) it shall have been made public by an act or omission of a party other than himself: (b) ARTIST receives such Confidential Information from an un-

related third party on a non-confidential basis; or (c) the passage of ten (10) years from the date of the disclosure of such Confidential Information to ARTIST, whichever shall first occur.

2.   ARTIST further agrees to use all reasonable precautions to assure that all such Confidential Information is properly protected and kept from unauthorized persons or disclosure.

3.   If requested by MANUFACTURER, ARTIST agrees to promptly return to MANUFACTURER all materials, writings, equipment, models, mechanisms and the like obtained from or through MANUFACTURER including, but not limited to, all Confidential Information, all of which ARTIST recognizes is the sole and exclusive property of MANUFACTURER;

4.   ARTIST agrees that he will not, without first obtaining the prior written permission of MANUFACTURER: (a) directly or indirectly utilize such Confidential Information in his own business; or (b) manufacture and/or sell any product which is based in whole or in part on such Confidential Information; or (c) disclosure such Confidential Information to any third party.

6. Warranty and Representation

(A)   ARTIST represents and warrants to MANUFACTURER that he is not a party to or otherwise bound by any agreement which may, in any way, restrict its right or ability to enter into this Agreement.

(B)   ARTIST agrees that he will not reveal to MANUFACTURER or otherwise utilize in his employment with MANUFACTURER any proprietary trade secrets or confidential information of any previous employer.

(C)   ARTIST represents and warrants that the Work Product which it creates on behalf of MANU-FACTURER shall be original and unique and does not infringe upon the rights of any third party.

7. Indemnity

ARTIST agrees to defend, indemnify and hold MANUFACTURER, its officers, directors, agents and employees harmless against all costs, expenses and losses (including reasonable attorneys' fees and costs) incurred through claims of third parties against MANUFACTURER based on a breach by ARTIST of any representation and warranty made in this Agreement.

8. Termination

Either party may terminate this Agreement on thirty (30) days written notice to the other party in the event of a breach of any provision of this Agreement by the other party, provided that, during the thirty (30) days period, the breaching party fails to cure such breach.

9. Jurisdiction and Disputes

This Agreement shall be governed by the laws of New York and all disputes hereunder shall be resolved in the applicable state or federal courts of New York. The parties consent to the jurisdiction of such courts, agree to accept service of process by mail and waive any jurisdictional or venue defenses otherwise available.

10. Agreement Binding on Successors

This Agreement shall be binding upon and shall inure to the benefit of the parties hereto, their heirs, administrators, successors and assigns.

11. Assignability

This Agreement and the rights and obligations thereunder with respect to ARTIST are personal to ARTIST and may not be assigned by any act of ARTIST or by operation of law without the prior written consent of MANUFACTURER. MANUFACTURER shall have the unfettered right to assign this Agreement to the purchaser of the assets of MANUFACTURER.

12. Waiver

No waiver by either party of any default shall be deemed as a waiver of any prior or subsequent default of the same or other provisions of this Agreement.

13. Severability

If any provision hereof is held invalid or unenforceable by a court of competent jurisdiction, such invalidity shall not affect the validity or operation of any other provision and such invalid provision shall be deemed to be severed from the Agreement.

14. Integration

This Agreement constitutes the entire understanding of the parties and revokes and supersedes all prior agreements between the parties and is intended as a final expression of their Agreement. It shall not be modified or amended except in writing signed by the parties hereto and specifically referring to this Agreement. This Agreement shall take precedence over any other documents which may be in conflict therewith.

IN WITNESS WHEREOF, the parties hereto, intending to be legally bound hereby, have each caused to be affixed hereto its or his/her hand and seal the day indicated.

MANUFACTURER   **ARTIST**

By: _____   By: _____

Date: _____   Date: _____

SCHEDULE A

Project(s): _____

_____

Title: _____

Task: Creation of packaging artwork for use by MANUFACTURER for _____.

Schedule:
Preliminary artwork to be submitted by
_____;

Final artwork to be submitted by
_____.

Royalty: _____

APPENDIX SIX:
Sample Release for Submission of Outside Concepts and Artwork

_____ (MANUFACTURER)
welcomes the submission of new concepts, artwork, ideas, or inventions from persons outside
the organization to which we will give careful consideration.

As MANUFACTURER is also in the business
of developing its own artwork and concepts as well
as regularly contracting with third parties, there
may be an occasion when we receive a submission which is similar to artwork or concepts which
we are working on ourselves or have licensed from
another party. It is, therefore, necessary that we
clearly establish our relationship at the outset.

In order to avoid any misunderstandings and
to protect our own development efforts, it is our
policy to accept and evaluate all disclosures of artwork and concepts on the following basis:

(1)   You agree to disclose the artwork or concept described in the attached Appendix A and all
information pertaining to such artwork or concept

(the "Property") to permit MANUFACTURER to evaluate same.

(2)   All submissions made by you are on a voluntary and unsolicited basis.

(3)   No confidential relationship is to be established between us as a result of your submission or from MANUFACTURER's consideration of the Property. Thus, you should understand that we will not retain your Property "in confidence." Confidential relationships have been held to create obligations and liabilities which are beyond what MANUFACTURER is willing to assume.

(4)   No obligation of any kind is assumed or may be implied against MANUFACTURER until a formal written agreement between us is signed and then the obligation will only be as defined by the terms of such agreement.

(5)   MANUFACTURER will honor and respect any intellectual property rights (e.g., patents, trademarks and copyrights) which you have for the Property. Your sole remedy arising out of your submission to MANUFACTURER, however, shall be limited to claims based on these intellectual property rights and you hereby waive any other claims.

(6)   You warrant that you are the sole and exclusive owner of the Property and that you are able to disclose the Property and related ideas and/or other suggestions to MANUFACTURER without violating or infringing the rights of any other per-

son or company. You agree to defend and indemnify MANUFACTURER for any action based on a breach of this warranty.

If the above letter is acceptable to you, kindly sign this letter and return it to us with a *description of your Property* for our consideration. We look forward to working with you in the future.

Agreed to and accepted:

_____
Signature

Print Name: _____
Address: _____
Date: _____

Appendix A

(Description of the Property)

APPENDIX SEVEN:
Sample License Agreement
Flat Fee

THIS AGREEMENT is entered into this _____ day of _____, 199_____, by and between _____, whose address is _____ ("ARTIST") and _____, a _____ corporation, with offices at _____ _____ ("MANUFACTURER").

WITNESSETH:

WHEREAS, ARTIST is the sole and exclusive owner of the copyrights, copyright registrations and works of art set forth in Schedule A attached hereto (the "Copyrights"); and

WHEREAS, ARTIST has the power and authority to grant to MANUFACTURER the right, privilege and license to reproduce, use, manufacture and sell derivative works of the Copyrights in the form and quantity as identified in Schedule A attached hereto (the "Licensed Products"); and

WHEREAS, MANUFACTURER desires to obtain from ARTIST an exclusive license to reproduce, use, manufacture, have manufactured, distribute and sell Licensed Products in the countries identified in Schedule A attached hereto (the "Licensed Territory"); and

WHEREAS, both MANUFACTURER and ARTIST have agreed to the terms and conditions upon which MANUFACTURER shall use, manufacture, have manufactured and sell Licensed Products.

NOW, THEREFORE, in consideration of the promises and agreements set forth herein, the parties, each intending to be legally bound hereby, do promise and agree as follows:

1. License

(A)   ARTIST hereby grants to MANUFACTURER for the Term of this Agreement as recited herein the exclusive right and license to reproduce, use, manufacture, distribute and sell the Licensed Products in the Licensed Territory. ARTIST also grants MANUFACTURER for the Term of this Agreement a license to utilize the Copyrights in promotional, packaging and advertising material used in the sale and distribution of the Licensed Products. The license granted hereunder includes a license under all copyright registrations and any applications therefore with respect to the Copyrights.

(B)   ARTIST agrees to allow MANUFACTURER, from time to time and at MANUFACTURER's request, access to and/or temporary possession of the original work incorporating the licensed Copyrights in order to facilitate the production of Licensed Products and/or promotional material used in support thereof.

2. Term

This Agreement shall be effective as of the date of execution by both parties and shall extend for Five (5) years (the "Term"), unless terminated earlier as provided herein.

3. Compensation

(A)   In consideration for the license granted hereunder, MANUFACTURER agrees to pay to ARTIST a one-time flat fee of the amount recited in Schedule A (the "Fee") due upon execution of this Agreement.

(B)   ARTIST's agreed-to compensation as provided for in Schedule A will be full payment for ARTIST, and ARTIST will not be entitled to any royalties or proceeds received by MANUFACTURER from the sale of the Licensed Products.

4. Warranties

(A)   ARTIST represents and warrants that it has the right and power to grant the licenses granted herein and that there are no other agreements with any other party in conflict with such grant.

(B)   ARTIST further represents and warrants that the Copyrights do not infringe any valid rights of any third party.

5. Notices, Quality Control and Samples

(A)   The License granted hereunder is conditioned upon MANUFACTURER's full and complete compliance with the marking provisions of the trademark and copyright laws of the United States.

(B)   The Licensed Products, as well as all promotional, packaging and advertising material relative thereto, shall include all appropriate legal notices as required by ARTIST, and shall, at the minimum, include the statutory copyright symbol, together with the year of publication of the work in question and the name of ARTIST.

(C)   The Licensed Products shall be of a high quality which is at least equal to comparable products manufactured and marketed by MANUFACTURER.

(D)   At least once during each calendar year, MANUFACTURER shall submit to ARTIST three (3) samples of Licensed Products.

6. Intellectual Property

(A)   MANUFACTURER acknowledges ARTIST's exclusive rights in the Copyrights and that ARTIST is the owner thereof.

(B)   It is understood and agreed that ARTIST shall retain all right, title and interest in the original Copyrights and, except as provided for herein, to any derivative works or modifications made from or to the Copyrights by MANUFACTURER.

(C)   At MANUFACTURER's request, ARTIST will provide MANUFACTURER with copies of all copyright registration certificates with respect to the licensed Copyrights. In the event that ARTIST has not applied for registration for the Copyrights with the U.S. Register of Copyrights, MANUFAC-TURER may request that it do so, at ARTIST's expense.

(D)   The parties agree to execute any documents reasonably requested by the other party to effect any of the above provisions.

7. Termination

(A)   MANUFACTURER shall have the right to terminate this Agreement at any time on sixty (60) days' written notice to ARTIST, such termination to become effective at the conclusion of such sixty (60) day period.

(B)   Either party may terminate this Agreement on thirty (30) days' written notice to the other party in the event of a breach of any provision of this Agreement by the other party, provided that, during the thirty (30) day period, the breaching party fails to cure such breach.

(C)   Upon the expiration or termination of this Agreement, unless otherwise provided for elsewhere herein, all of the rights of MANUFACTURER under this Agreement shall forthwith terminate and immediately revert to ARTIST, and MANUFACTURER shall immediately discontinue all use of the Copyrights.

8. Post-Termination Rights and Obligations

(A)   Not less than thirty (30) days prior to the expiration of this Agreement or immediately upon termination thereof, MANUFACTURER shall provide ARTIST with a complete schedule of all inventory of Licensed Products then on-hand (the "Inventory").

(B)   Upon expiration or termination of this Agreement before the end of the term, except for reason of a breach of MANUFACTURER's duty to comply with legal notice marking requirements, MANUFACTURER shall be entitled, for three (3) months (the "Sell-Off Period"), on an exclusive basis, to continue to sell such Inventory. Such sales shall be made subject to all the provisions of this Agreement. At the conclusion of the Sell-Off Period, ARTIST shall have the option to purchase the Inventory from MANUFACTURER at a price equal to fifty percent (50%) of MANUFACTURER's Net Selling Price.

(C)   Upon expiration or termination of this Agreement, ARTIST may require that the MANUFACTURER transmit to ARTIST, at no cost, all material relating to the Copyrights including all artwork, color separations and the like.

(D) Upon expiration or termination of this Agreement, except for reason of a breach of this Agreement by MANUFACTURER, ARTIST hereby agrees that it shall not manufacture, sell and/or distribute Licensed Products, nor grant a license or assignment to any third party to manufacture, sell and/or distribute Licensed Product incorporating, based upon or derived from the Copyrights for a period of Five (5) years from the date of termination or expiration. MANUFACTURER shall, however, have the right to sell those Licensed Products purchased from ARTIST pursuant to subparagraph 8(B), above.

9. Indemnity

(A) ARTIST agrees to defend, indemnify and hold MANUFACTURER, its officers, directors, agents and employees, harmless against all costs, expenses and losses (including reasonable attorneys' fees and costs) incurred through claims of third parties against MANUFACTURER based on a breach by ARTIST of any representation and warranty made in this Agreement.

(B) MANUFACTURER agrees to defend and indemnify ARTIST, its officers, directors, agents and employees, against all costs, expenses and losses (including reasonable attorneys' fees and costs) incurred through claims of third parties against ARTIST based on the manufacturer or sale of the Licensed Products under the Copyrights.

10. Infringements

(A)   ARTIST shall have the right, in its sole discretion, to prosecute lawsuits against third persons for infringement of ARTIST's rights in the Property. If ARTIST does not institute an infringement suit within thirty (30) days after MANUFACTURER's written request that it do so, MANUFACTURER may institute and prosecute such lawsuit in its own name and/or on behalf of ARTIST.

(B)   Any lawsuit shall be prosecuted solely at the expense of the party bringing suit and all sums recovered shall be retained by the party bringing suit.

(C)   The parties agree to fully cooperate with the other party in the prosecution of any such suit. The party bringing suit shall reimburse the other party for the expenses incurred as a result of such cooperation.

11. Notices

Any notice required to be given pursuant to this Agreement shall be in writing and mailed by certified or registered mail, return receipt requested, by telex, telefax or telegram, or delivered by a national overnight express service.

12. Jurisdiction

This Agreement shall be governed in accordance with the laws of the United States and the State of New York, and all disputes under this Agreement shall be resolved by the applicable state or federal courts of New York. The parties hereby accept the jurisdiction of such courts, agree to accept service of process by mail, and hereby waive any jurisdictional or venue defenses otherwise available.

13. Agreement Binding on Successors

The provisions of the Agreement shall be binding upon and shall inure to the benefit of the parties hereto, their heirs, administrators, successors and assigns.

14. Assignability

The license granted hereunder may be assignable by MANUFACTURER upon thirty (30) days' written notice to ARTIST. MANUFACTURER shall have no authority, however, to assign its obligations under this Agreement without express written approval by ARTIST.

15. Waiver

No waiver by either party of any default shall be deemed as a waiver of prior or subsequent default of the same or other provisions of this Agreement.

16. Severability

If any term, clause or provision hereof is held invalid or unenforceable by a court of competent jurisdiction, such invalidity shall not affect the validity or operation of any other term, clause or provision and such invalid term, clause or provision shall be deemed to be severed from the Agreement.

17. Integration

This Agreement constitutes the entire understanding of the parties, and revokes and supersedes all prior agreements between the parties. It shall not be modified or amended except in writing signed by the parties hereto and specifically referring to this Agreement.

IN WITNESS WHEREOF, the parties hereto, intending to be legally bound hereby, have each caused to be affixed hereto its or his/her hand and seal the day indicated.

ARTIST   MANUFACTURER

By: _____   By: _____
Date: _____   Date: _____

SCHEDULE A

Artist: _____

Artist Address: _____

_____

Artist Telephone: _____

Artist Telefax: _____

1. Copyrights

The following Copyrights form part of this Agreement:

Title of Work   Copyright Registration No.

(Attach photographs if necessary to identify the licensed works on Exhibit A attached hereto).

2. Licensed Products

The Licensed Products are as follows:

(List Categories of Licensed Products)

3. Licensed Territory

The following countries shall constitute the Licensed Territory:

(i.e., U.S. and its possessions, Worldwide)

4. Royalty Rate

The Royalty Rate is as follows:

_____ percent (___%)

EXHIBIT A

(Attach photographs of licensed works)

Sample License Agreement
Royalty-Based

THIS AGREEMENT is entered into this _____ day of _____, 199_____, by and between _____, whose address is _____ ("ARTIST") and _____, a _____ corporation, with offices at _____ _____ ("MANUFACTURER").

WITNESSETH:

WHEREAS, ARTIST is the sole and exclusive owner of the copyrights, copyright registrations and works of art set forth in Schedule A attached hereto (the "Copyrights"); and

WHEREAS, ARTIST has the power and authority to grant to MANUFACTURER the right, privilege and license to reproduce, use, manufacture and sell derivative works of the Copyrights in the form and quantity as identified in Schedule A attached hereto (the "Licensed Products"); and

WHEREAS, MANUFACTURER desires to obtain from ARTIST an exclusive license to reproduce, use, manufacture, have manufactured, distribute and sell Licensed Products in the countries identified in Schedule A attached hereto (the "Licensed Territory"); and

WHEREAS, both MANUFACTURER and ARTIST have agreed to the terms and conditions upon which MANUFACTURER shall use, manufacture, have manufactured and sell Licensed Products.

NOW, THEREFORE, in consideration of the promises and agreements set forth herein, the parties, each intending to be legally bound hereby, do promise and agree as follows:

1. License

(A)   ARTIST hereby grants to MANUFACTURER for the Term of this Agreement as recited herein the exclusive right and license to reproduce, use, manufacture, distribute and sell the Licensed Products in the Licensed Territory. ARTIST also grants MANUFACTURER for the Term of this Agreement a license to utilize the Copyrights in promotional, packaging and advertising material used in the sale and distribution of the Licensed Products. The license granted hereunder includes a license under all copyright registrations and any applications therefore with respect to the Copyrights.

(B)   ARTIST agrees to allow MANUFACTURER, from time to time and at MANUFACTURER's request, access to and/or temporary possession of the original work incorporating the licensed Copyrights in order to facilitate the production of Licensed Products and/or promotional material used in support thereof.

2. Term

This Agreement shall be effective as of the date of execution by both parties and shall extend for Five (5) years (the "Term"), unless terminated earlier as provided herein.

3. Compensation

(A)   In consideration for the license granted hereunder, MANUFACTURER agrees to pay to ARTIST the royalty recited in Schedule A (the "Royalty") based on MANUFACTURER's Net Sales of Licensed Products.

(B)   The Royalty owed ARTIST shall be calculated on a quarterly calendar basis (the "Royalty Period") and shall be payable no later than thirty (30) days after the termination of the preceding full calendar quarter, i.e., commencing on the first (1st) day of January, April, July and October, except that the first and last calendar quarters may be "short" depending on the effective date of this Agreement.

(C)   For each Royalty Period, MANUFACTURER shall provide ARTIST with a written royalty statement reciting, on a design-by-design basis, the number of units sold, quantity shipped, gross invoice, amount billed customers less discounts, allowances and returns.

(D) "Net Sales" shall mean MANUFAC-TURER's gross sales (the gross invoice amount billed customers) of Licensed Products, less discounts and allowances actually shown on the invoice and, further, less any bona fide returns (net of all returns actually made or allowed as supported by credit memoranda actually issued to the customers) up to the amount of the actual sales of the Licensed Products during the Royalty Period.

(E) MANUFACTURER's obligations for the payment of Royalties shall survive expiration or termination of this Agreement and will continue for so long as MANUFACTURER continues to sell the Licensed Products.

4. Warranties

(A) ARTIST represents and warrants that it has the right and power to grant the licenses granted herein and that there are no other agreements with any other party in conflict with such grant.

(B) ARTIST further represents and warrants that the Copyrights do not infringe any valid rights of any third party.

5. Notices, Quality Control and Samples

(A)   The License granted hereunder is conditioned upon MANUFACTURER's full and complete compliance with the marking provisions of the trademark and copyright laws of the United States.

(B)   The Licensed Products, as well as all promotional, packaging and advertising material relative thereto, shall include all appropriate legal notices as required by ARTIST, and shall, at the minimum, include the statutory copyright symbol, together with the year of publication of the work in question and the name of ARTIST.

(C)   The Licensed Products shall be of a high quality which is at least equal to comparable products manufactured and marketed by MANUFACTURER.

(D)   At least once during each calendar year, MANUFACTURER shall submit to ARTIST three (3) samples of Licensed Products.

6. Intellectual Property

(A)   MANUFACTURER acknowledges ARTIST's exclusive rights in the Copyrights and that ARTIST is the owner thereof.

(B)   It is understood and agreed that ARTIST shall retain all right, title and interest in the original Copyrights and, except as provided for herein, to any derivative works or modifications made from or to the Copyrights by MANUFACTURER.

(C)   At MANUFACTURER's request, ARTIST will provide MANUFACTURER with copies of all copyright registration certificates with respect to the licensed Copyrights. In the event that ARTIST has not applied for registration for the Copyrights with the U.S. Register of Copyrights, MANUFAC-TURER may request that it do so, at ARTIST's expense.

(D)   The parties agree to execute any documents reasonably requested by the other party to effect any of the above provisions.

7. Termination

(A)   MANUFACTURER shall have the right to terminate this Agreement at any time on sixty (60) days' written notice to ARTIST, such termination to become effective at the conclusion of such sixty (60) day period.

(B)   Either party may terminate this Agreement on thirty (30) days' written notice to the other party in the event of a breach of any provision of this Agreement by the other party, provided that, during the thirty (30) day period, the breaching party fails to cure such breach.

(C)   Upon the expiration or termination of this Agreement, unless otherwise provided for elsewhere herein, all of the rights of MANUFACTURER under this Agreement shall forthwith terminate and immediately revert to ARTIST, and MANUFAC-TURER shall immediately discontinue all use of the Copyrights.

8. Post-Termination Rights and Obligations

(A)   Not less than thirty (30) days prior to the expiration of this Agreement or immediately upon termination thereof, MANUFACTURER shall pro-vide ARTIST with a complete schedule of all in-ventory of Licensed Products then on-hand (the "Inventory").

(B)   Upon expiration or termination of this Agreement before the end of the term, except for reason of a breach of MANUFACTURER's duty to comply with legal notice marking requirements, MANUFACTURER shall be entitled, for three (3) months (the "Sell-Off Period"), on an exclusive basis, to continue to sell such Inventory. Such sales shall be made subject to all the provisions of this Agreement including the payment of a Roy-alty which shall be due within thirty (30) days af-ter the close of the Sell-Off period. At the conclu-sion of the Sell-Off Period, ARTIST shall have the option to purchase it from MANUFACTURER at a price equal to fifty percent (50%) of MANUFACTURER's Net Selling Price.

(C)   Upon expiration or termination of this Agreement, ARTIST may require that the MANU-FACTURER transmit to ARTIST, at no cost, all material relating to the Copyrights including all artwork, color separations and the like.

(D)   Upon expiration or termination of this Agreement, except for reason of a breach of this Agreement by MANUFACTURER, ARTIST hereby agrees that it shall not manufacture, sell and/or distribute Licensed Products, nor grant a license or assignment to any third party to manufacture, sell and/or distribute Licensed Product incorporating, based upon or derived from the Copyrights for a period of Five (5) years from the date of termination or expiration. MANUFACTURER shall, however, have the right to sell those Licensed Products purchased from ARTIST pursuant to subparagraph 8(B), above.

9. Indemnity

(A)   ARTIST agrees to defend, indemnify and hold MANUFACTURER, its officers, directors, agents and employees, harmless against all costs, expenses and losses (including reasonable attorneys' fees and costs) incurred through claims of third parties against MANUFACTURER based on a breach by ARTIST of any representation and warranty made in this Agreement.

(B)   MANUFACTURER agrees to defend and indemnify ARTIST, its officers, directors, agents and employees, against all costs, expenses and losses (including reasonable attorneys' fees and costs) incurred through claims of third parties against ARTIST based on the manufacturer or sale of the Licensed Products under the Copyrights.

10. Infringements

(A) ARTIST shall have the right, in its sole discretion, to prosecute lawsuits against third persons for infringement of ARTIST's rights in the Property. If ARTIST does not institute an infringement suit within thirty (30) days after MANUFACTURER's written request that it do so, MANUFACTURER may institute and prosecute such lawsuit in its own name and/or on behalf of ARTIST.

(B) Any lawsuit shall be prosecuted solely at the expense of the party bringing suit and all sums recovered shall be retained by the party bringing suit.

(C) The parties agree to fully cooperate with the other party in the prosecution of any such suit. The party bringing suit shall reimburse the other party for the expenses incurred as a result of such cooperation.

11. Notices

Any notice required to be given pursuant to this Agreement shall be in writing and mailed by certified or registered mail, return receipt requested, by telex, telefax or telegram, or delivered by a national overnight express service.

12. Jurisdiction

This Agreement shall be governed in accordance with the laws of the United States and the State of _____, and all disputes under this Agreement shall be resolved by the applicable state or federal courts of _____. The parties hereby accept the jurisdiction of such courts, agree to accept service of process by mail, and hereby waive any jurisdictional or venue defenses otherwise available.

13. Agreement Binding on Successors

The provisions of the Agreement shall be binding upon and shall inure to the benefit of the parties hereto, their heirs, administrators, successors and assigns.

14. Assignability

The license granted hereunder may be assignable by MANUFACTURER upon thirty (30) days' written notice to ARTIST. MANUFACTURER shall have no authority, however, to assign its obligations under this Agreement without express written approval by ARTIST.

15. Waiver

No waiver by either party of any default shall be deemed as a waiver of prior or subsequent default of the same or other provisions of this Agreement.

16. Severability

If any term, clause or provision hereof is held invalid or unenforceable by a court of competent jurisdiction, such invalidity shall not affect the validity or operation of any other term, clause or provision and such invalid term, clause or provision shall be deemed to be severed from the Agreement.

17. Integration

This Agreement constitutes the entire understanding of the parties, and revokes and supersedes all prior agreements between the parties. It shall not be modified or amended except in writing signed by the parties hereto and specifically referring to this Agreement.

IN WITNESS WHEREOF, the parties hereto, intending to be legally bound hereby, have each caused to be affixed hereto its or his/her hand and seal the day indicated.

ARTIST   **MANUFACTURER**

By: _____   By: _____
Date: _____   Date: _____

SCHEDULE A

Artist: _____

Artist Address: _____

_____

Artist Telephone: _____

Artist Telefax: _____

1. Copyrights

The following Copyrights form part of this Agreement:

Title of Work   Copyright Registration No.

2. Licensed Products

The Licensed Products are as follows:

3. Licensed Territory

The following countries shall constitute the Licensed Territory:

_____

4. Royalty Rate

The Royalty Rate is as follows:

EXHIBIT A

(Attach photographs of licensed works)

Sample Agent Agreement

THIS AGREEMENT is made this _____ day of
_____, 199 _____ by and between
_____, a _____ corporation
with offices at _____
_____ ("AGENT") and
_____ with offices at _____
_____ (the "ARTIST").

WITNESSETH:

WHEREAS, the ARTIST is in the business of and
has developed certain patterns, designs, artwork,
products and intellectual property identified more
fully in the attached Exhibit A (the "Works");

WHEREAS, the ARTIST is desirous of retaining the services of an experienced licensing agent
to commercialize or otherwise license the Works
to third party manufacturers (the "Manufacturer")
for a line of licensed products (the "Licensed Products"); and

WHEREAS, AGENT is willing to represent the
ARTIST with respect to commercialization of the
Works;

NOW, THEREFORE, in consideration of the promises and agreements set forth herein, the parties, each intending to be legally bound hereby, do promise and agree as follows:

1. Agent Grant

(A)   The ARTIST hereby grants to AGENT, during the Term of this Agreement, the exclusive right (to the exclusion of others and of the ARTIST representing itself) to represent the ARTIST in the following countries:

_____

_____

(the "Territory") with respect to the commercialization or licensing of the Works to Manufacturers.

(B)   With respect to agreements with Manufacturers, ARTIST hereby empowers the AGENT to negotiate the terms of such agreements and to execute such agreements on behalf of the ARTIST as its agent. All such agreements shall be in the joint names of the AGENT and the ARTIST and shall utilize a form agreement which has been previously approved by the ARTIST.

(C)   In the event that the ARTIST is approached directly by a manufacturer within the Territory during the Term of this Agreement, it shall refer such manufacturer to the AGENT. ARTIST agrees that during the Term of this Agreement, it will not negotiate with any other person or entity within the Territory to represent it in any capacity in connection with the manufacture or sale of the Works.

2. Term of the Agreement

(A)   This Agreement and the provisions hereof, except as otherwise provided, shall be in full force and effect commencing on the date of execution by both parties and shall extend for a Term of two (2) years thereafter (the "Term"). This Agreement shall be automatically renewed for additional one (1) year "Extended Terms" unless either party notifies the other in writing of its intention not to renew the Agreement, such notification to be provided at least sixty (60) days prior to the expiration of the then in-effect Term.

(B)   In the event that AGENT is successful in commercializing the Works with a Third Party Manufacturer during the Term of this Agreement, this Agreement shall be automatically extended to run concurrently with the term of any agreement with such Manufacturer.

3. Duties and Obligations

(A)   Subject to the conditions herein specified, AGENT shall use its best efforts during the Term of this Agreement to find and conclude business arrangements with Manufacturers which are advantageous to the ARTIST for the Works.

(B)   AGENT agrees to consult with and keep ARTIST reasonably informed as negotiations develop. ARTIST shall have the right to disapprove negotiations with any particular Manufacturer.

(C)   AGENT shall, from time to time, when requested by ARTIST, discuss with ARTIST potential licenses, product categories, possible markets and the like for planning purposes.

(D)   AGENT acknowledges the existence of confidential relationships between ARTIST and outside artists who may be the creators of a portion of the Works hereof. AGENT agrees that it will not during the Term of this Agreement or for a period of one (1) year after termination or expiration thereof, contact such artists for purposes of representation.

(E)   ARTIST shall have the full and total control over its trademarks and the use thereof. AGENT shall use its best efforts to insure that provisions shall be contained in all agreements with third party Manufacturers affording ARTIST the right to make quality inspections at any place and at any reasonable time to insure that the quality is being maintained and that the Manufacturers agree to utilize proper trademark and copyright notices on all such Works.

(F)   It is understood that the ARTIST may have concepts and properties other than the aforementioned Works and such concepts and properties do not form part of this Agreement. ARTIST may not, either directly or indirectly during the Term of this Agreement or for a period of one (1) year thereafter, commercialize such concepts or properties with any manufacturer introduced to ARTIST by AGENT during the Term of this Agreement.

In the event that ARTIST shall enter into any such agreement with any such manufacturer for any such concept or properties, such concept or properties shall be automatically added to this Agreement.

(G)   All decisions to supply film or other materials to a particular Manufacturer shall be made by the ARTIST.

(H)   It is understood that AGENT may render similar services for other clients and/or continue to develop properties of its own and license or sell such properties to Manufacturers. Nothing contained in this Agreement shall preclude AGENT from rendering such services or continuing to develop and sell or license such properties.

4. Compensation

(A)   In full consideration for the services rendered by AGENT, the ARTIST agrees to and shall pay AGENT a Commission of _____ percent (_____%) of the Net Revenues received by the ARTIST from the Manufacturer for the Works.

(B)   "Net Revenues" shall include all income received by the ARTIST (prior to the deduction of

AGENT's commission) from such third party Manufacturers within the Territory pursuant to any contract or agreement for the sale, lease, license or other disposition of the Works resulting directly from the efforts of AGENT including, but not limited to, advances, royalties, guarantees, fees and payments less any payments made or expenses incurred by AGENT for or on behalf of the ARTIST with the prior approval of ARTIST.

(C)   After termination or expiration of this Agreement for any reason, AGENT shall be entitled to continue to receive its full Commission based on contracts or agreements entered into by ARTIST with Manufacturers in the Territory during the Term of this Agreement or based on any contracts or agreements entered into by ARTIST within one (1) year from the date of termination or expiration thereof resulting from presentations or negotiations made by AGENT during the Term of this Agreement for which AGENT would have received a commission had the Agreement not been terminated or expired. AGENT shall be entitled to such post-termination Commission for so long as the ARTIST receives revenues under such agreements and any renewals, modifications or extensions thereof.

5. Warranties and Indemnifications

(A)   The ARTIST represents and warrants that it is the owner of all rights in and to the Works, that it has the right and power to license and/or sell such Works, that the use of the Works on the

Licensed Products shall not infringe upon the rights of any third party, and that it has not granted anyone else the right or authority to act for it in a manner which would conflict with AGENT.

(B) The ARTIST hereby agrees to defend, indemnify and hold AGENT, its shareholders, directors, officers, employees, agents, parent companies, subsidiaries and affiliates, harmless from and against any and all claims, liabilities, judgments, penalties, and taxes, civil and criminal, and all costs and expenses (including, without limitation, reasonable attorneys' fees) incurred in connection therewith, which any of them may incur or to which any of them may be subjected, arising out of or relating to a breach of the ARTIST's representations and warranties. During the pendency of any indemnified claim against the AGENT, AGENT shall have the right to withhold any monies then owed ARTIST to help defray any costs or expenses that ARTIST may incur as a result of such claim.

(C) AGENT hereby agrees to defend, indemnify and hold the ARTIST, their shareholders, directors, officers, employees, agents, parent companies, subsidiaries, and affiliates, harmless from and against any and all claims, liabilities, judgments, penalties, and taxes, civil and criminal, and all costs and expenses (including, without limitation, reasonable attorneys' fees) incurred in connection therewith, which any of them may incur or to which any of them may be subjected, arising out of or relating to any action by AGENT.

143

6. Statements and Payments

(A)   AGENT shall receive all royalty reports and collect all royalties and payments from the Manufacturers both during and after termination or expiration of this Agreement. Such royalties and payments shall be deposited in an account which the parties mutually agree upon.

(B)   The AGENT agrees to keep accurate books of account and records at its principal place of business, covering all transactions relating to the agreements with the Manufacturers. ARTIST, through an independent certified public accountant acceptable to the AGENT, shall have the right, at all reasonable hours of the day and upon at least ten (10) business days' notice, to examine the AGENT's books and records as they relate to the subject matter of this Agreement only. Such examination shall occur at the place where the AGENT maintains such records.

(C)   All books and records pertaining to the obligations of the ARTIST hereunder shall be maintained and kept accessible and available to AGENT for inspection for at least one (1) year after the date to which they pertain.

7. Notice and Payment

(A)   Any notice required to be given under this Agreement shall be in writing and delivered personally to the other designated party at the above stated address or mailed by certified, registered or

Express mail, return receipt requested or by Federal Express.

(B)   Either party may change the address to which notice or payment is to be sent by written notice to the other under any provision of this paragraph.

8. Termination

This Agreement may be terminated by either party upon thirty (30) days' written notice to the other party in the event of a breach of a material provision of this Agreement by the other party, provided that, during the thirty (30) day period, the breaching party fails to cure such breach.

9. Effect of Termination

(A)   Upon termination or expiration of this Agreement as it relates to the Works, all rights granted to AGENT relative to the Works shall forthwith revert to the ARTIST who shall be free to contract with others to commercialize such Works subject to the provisions of this Agreement subject to the post-termination provisions of this Agreement. AGENT shall, thereafter, refrain from further efforts to commercialize the Works.

(B)   Upon termination or expiration of this Agreement, ARTIST may request that the AGENT provide it within sixty (60) days of such notice with a complete schedule of all prospective Manufacturers contacted on behalf of the ARTIST relative to the Works as well as returning all artwork and promotional material relating to the Works.

10. Jurisdiction/Disputes

This Agreement shall be governed in accordance with the laws of the State of _____. All disputes under this Agreement shall be resolved by litigation in the courts of the State of _____ and the parties all consent to the jurisdiction of such courts, agree to accept service of process by mail, and hereby waive any jurisdictional or venue defenses otherwise available to it.

11. Agreement Binding on Successors

The provisions of the Agreement shall be binding upon and shall inure to the benefit of the parties hereto, their heirs, administrators, successors and assigns.

12. Assignability

Neither party may assign this Agreement or the rights and obligations thereunder to any third party without the prior express written approval of the other party which shall not be unreasonably withheld.

13. Waiver

No waiver by either party of any default shall be deemed as a waiver of prior or subsequent default of the same or other provisions of this Agreement.

14. Severability

If any term, clause or provision hereof is held invalid or unenforceable by a court of competent jurisdiction, such invalidity shall not affect the validity or operation of any other term, clause or provision and such invalid term, clause or provision shall be deemed to be severed from the Agreement.

15. Independent Contractor

AGENT shall be deemed an independent contractor and nothing contained herein shall constitute this arrangement to be employment, a joint venture or a partnership. AGENT shall be solely responsible for and shall hold the ARTIST harmless from any and all claims for taxes, fees or costs, including but not limited to withholding, income tax, FICA, workman's compensation.

16. Integration

This Agreement constitutes the entire understanding of the parties, and revokes and supersedes all prior agreements between the parties and is intended as a final expression of their Agreement. It shall not be modified or amended except in writing signed by the parties hereto and specifically referring to this Agreement. This Agreement shall take precedence over any other documents which may conflict with this Agreement.

IN WITNESS WHEREOF, the parties hereto, intending to be legally bound hereby, have each caused to be affixed hereto its or his/her hand and seal the day indicated.

ARTIST   **AGENT**

By: _____   By: _____

Date: _____   Date: _____

SCHEDULE A

Works

APPENDIX TEN:
Listing of Possible Licensed Product Categories

Apparel
- Boys
- Girls
- Holiday
- Infant
- Men
- Sleepwear
- Sportswear
- Teen
- Underwear
- Women

Bath Accessories
Board Games
Books
Calendars
Dinnerware
Figurines
Frames
Gift Bags
Gift Wrap
Greeting Cards
Handbags

Jewelry
Linens
Luggage
Needlecrafts
Paper Tableware
Phone Cards
Pillows
Plaques
Plates
Playing Cards
Postcards
Posters
Prints
Puzzles
Rugs
Scarves
Social Books (Address, Journals, Diaries)
Stationery
Stitchery
Textiles
Ties
Tiles

Tins/Boxes
Toys
Trading Cards
Wall Decor
Wallcoverings
Wallet Cards

Directory of Manufacturers: Alphabetical

Beach Products

One Paper Place
Kalamazoo, MI 49001
Telephone: 616-349-2626
Telefax: 616-349-6412
Barry Matus, V.P.-Creative & Marketing
Services

Dinnerware (Paper)	Gift Bags
Gift Wrap	Party Favors
Stationery	Tins/Boxes

Bertels Can Company

Route 115, P.O. Box 550
Effort, PA 18330
Telephone: 717-629-3938
Telefax: 717-629-4600
Ellen Hungarter, Art Director

Decorative Tapered Cans (ranging from 2 to 20 gallons)

Ceaco, Inc.
124 Watertown Street
Watertown, MA 02172
Telephone: 617-926-8080
Telefax: 617-924-7554
Lisa Casella, Art Director
Puzzles

Coastal Concepts, Inc.
1200 Avenida Chelsea
Vista, CA 92083
Telephone: 619-558-2501
Telefax: 619-558-2505
Skya Nelson, Art Director
Apparel-Teen

College Concepts Inc.
6445 Powers Ferry Road, Suite 330
Atlanta, GA 30339
Telephone: 770-859-1420
Telefax: 770-859-1434
Christine Zelt, License Coordinator
Apparel-Boys; Holiday; Men; Sleepwear; Sportswear; Teen; Underwear

Great American Puzzle Factory, Inc.
16 S. Main Street
South Norwalk, CT 06854
Telephone: 203-838-4240
Telefax: 203-838-2065
Anne Mulligan, Art Director
Board Games   Puzzles

Imperial Wallcoverings

23645 Mercantile Road

Cleveland, OH 44094

Telephone: 216-765-8763

Telefax: 216-292-3206

Lori Russell, Manager, Line Development/
Licensing
Wallcoverings

JCA, Inc.

35 Scales Lane

Townsend, MA 01469

Telephone: 508-597-8794

Telefax: 508-597-2632

Carrie Getz, Product Manager
Needlecrafts   Stitchery

Jillson & Roberts Gift Wrappings

5 Watson Avenue

Irving, CA 92718

Telephone: 714-859-8781

Telefax: 714-859-0259

John Newfeld, Art Director
Gift Bags   Gift Wrap

Jones & Mitchell Sportswear, Inc.

6800 West 153rd Street

Overland Park, KS 66223

Telephone: 913-897-5400

Telefax: 913-897-5448

Jenny Scott, Licensing Coordinator
Apparel-Sportswear

Majestic Athletic

636 Pen Argyl Street

Pen Argyl, PA 18017

Telephone: 610-863-6161

Telefax: 610-867-7006

Mark Shulman, Vice President,

Merchandising

Apparel-Boys; Men; Sportswear; Teen

MV Sport

88 Spence Street

Bay Shore, NY 11706

Telephone: 800-367-7900

Telefax: 516-435-8018

Gloria J. Driscoll, National Sales Manager

Apparel-Sportswear

Nalpac Ltd.

8700 Capital

Oak Park, MI 48237

Telephone: 810-541-1140

Telefax: 810-544-9126

Ralph Caplan, President

Board Games	Books
Calendars	Gift Wrap
Greeting Cards	Mugs
Pillows	Plaques
Playing Cards	Puzzles
T-shirts	Ties
Tins/Boxes	Toys
Wall Decor	

Pace Products, Inc.

333 Semoran Commerce Place
Apopka, FL 32703
Telephone: 407-880-2422
Telefax: 407-880-3467
Kris Patterson, Managing Editor
Books

Pacific Trading Cards Inc.

18424 Highway 99
Lynnwood, WA 98037
Telephone: 206-774-8473
Telefax: 206-775-0774
Michael Cramer, President
Trading Cards

Riegel Consumer Products

1 Riegel Road
Johnstown, SC 29832
Telephone: 800-845-3251
Telefax: 803-275-2219
Chris Cole, Merchandise Manager
Bedding   Textiles

Starline, Inc.

19-10 Hazen Street
E. Elmhurst, NY 11370
Telephone: 718-267-0600
Telefax: 718-267-1915
Martin D. Glick, Vice President, Sales
Calendars   Posters
Stationery

Sunburst Designs

100-B Woodwinds Industrial Court
Cary, NC 27511
Telephone: 919-481-4475
Telefax: 919-481-2522
Martha Wright/Gail Lehning, President/
Manager
Glass
Suncatchers to Hang in Windows
Tins/Boxes

Sunrise Publications, Inc.

1145 Sunrise Greeting Ct.
Bloomington, IN 47404
Telephone: 812-336-9900
Telefax: 812-336-8712
Artistic Resources Administrative Assistant

Frames	Gift Bags
Gift Wrap	Greeting Cards
Postcards	Posters
Prints	Social Books
Stationery	Tins/Boxes

Thunder Island

47 West 34th Street
New York, NY 10001
Telephone: 212-947-8855
Telefax: 212-947-8977
Michael Schoenfeld, Director of
Merchandising
Apparel: Boys, Girls, Holiday, Men, Sportswear and
Women

APPENDIX TWELVE:
Directory of Manufacturers by Product Category

Category	Manufacturer
Apparel	Coastal Concepts, Inc. College Concepts Inc. Jones & Mitchell Sportswear Majestic Athletic MV Sport Thunder Island
Board Games	Great American Puzzle Factory Nalpac Ltd.
Books	Nalpac Ltd. Pace Products
Calendars	Nalpac Ltd. Starline Inc.
Dinnerware (Paper)	Beach Products
Frames	Sunrise Publications, Inc.

Gift Bags	Beach Products Jillson & Roberts Gift Wrappings Sunrise Publications, Inc.
Gift Wrap	Beach Products Jillson & Roberts Gift Wrappings Nalpac Ltd. Sunrise Publications, Inc.
Greeting Cards	Nalpac Ltd. Sunrise Publications, Inc.
Needlecraft/ Stitchery	JCA, Inc.
Pillows	Nalpac Ltd.
Plaques	Nalpac Ltd.
Playing Cards	Nalpac Ltd.
Postcards	Sunrise Publications, Inc.
Posters/Prints	Sunrise Publications, Inc.
Puzzles	Ceaco, Inc. Great American Puzzle Factory Nalpac Ltd.
Social Books	Sunrise Publications, Inc.
Stationery	Beach Products Starline, Inc. Sunrise Publications, Inc.

Textiles	Riegel Consumer Products
Ties	Nalpac Ltd.
Tins/Boxes	Beach Products
	Nalpac Ltd.
	Sunburst Designs
	Sunrise Publications, Inc.
Toys	Nalpac Ltd.
Trading Cards	Pacific Trading Cards, Inc.
Wall Decor	Nalpac Ltd.
Wall Coverings	Imperial Wallcoverings

Index

-J-
Jurisdiction, 57

-L-
Legal notices, 55, 83
Levites, Gail, 30
License agreement
   flat fee, 113-124
   royalty-based, 125-136
Licensing Book, The, 22-23, 63, 87
Licensing Journal, The, 22, 63, 87
Licensing Letter, The, 63, 87
Licensing Today, 63
Licensing Trends, 63, 87

-M-
Manufacturers, 16, 151-159
Market channels, 19-21, 46
Marketing, 19-20

-N-
Net selling price, 51
Non-exclusive licenses, 45

-P-
Patents, 70, 71-73, 83
Presentation
   scope of, 30
   organizing, 31
   interview, 32-33
Product categories, 10, 14-15, 149-150

Product development
   chain, 21

-Q-
Quality control, 53

-R-
Records, 54
Release forms, 35, 109-111
Renewals, 48, 57
Representations in the license agreement, 55-56
Retailers, 25-26
Rights, 45
Royalty calculations, 51-52
Royalty reports, 54
Royalty-based agreements, 50, 99-108, 125-136

-S-
Samples, 54
Seminars, 26
Severability of the license agreement, 58
Sub-licensing, 48

-T-
Term of the agreement, 48, 65-66
Termination of the agreement, 57
Territory, 47
Trade publications, 22, 63, 86-88

Trade shows, 26-27, 88-90

Trademarks, 55, 69-70, 73-77, 82, 83

-U-

U.S. Patent and Trademark Office, 72, 75, 76, 77

-V-

VA form for copyrights, 79, 91-92

Verbal agreements, 39

-W-

Warranties in the license agreement, 55-56

Women's Wear Daily, 22, 88

Work for hire agreements
flat fee, 93-98
royalty-based, 99-108, 44, 48, 80, 93-108